FROM THE ASHES; SHE IS IGNITED

LOUISA HERRIDGE

CONTENTS

WELCOME INTRODUCTION

Welcome and thank you for buying this book. You are already ignited by taking this time for you... time to sit down, read and absorb the power of the stories being shared for you.

This is *more* than a book. These pages hold previously untold stories, secrets and hurts and in turn each chapter holds a piece of the author's heart. You will be taken on journeys of darkness, heartbreak, breakdowns, and despair which as a collective will help to guide you the reader and offer support and tools for anyone still in their own darkness to find the light and be ignited, like the authors all have.

This has been a collaborative and heart-led project bringing together women from across the globe with powerful stories to share. Stories of surviving and thriving. Stories of over-coming adversity. Stories of transcending pain and fear to live a full life. Stories of the *power* of women and how together we lift each other up. We don't just *rise* from the Ashes. We IGNITE.

'*From the Ashes; She is Ignited*' is the testament that any woman can overcome any darkness to find the fire and light of life!

FROM THE ASHES

Yes, we all know the tale of the phoenix rising from the ashes, but the idea for this book initially came from Greek Mythology and the story of Persephone. Captured and raped by Hades she was trapped in the underworld. Persephone was tempted by Hades to eat a pomegranate seed, the fruit of the underworld and so was condemned to a life in the underworld. Of course, being a woman meant that the sin was entirely hers!

The story of Persephone resonated with me because she is also known as the Goddess of spring. As the daughter of Zeus, he struck a deal with Hades meaning that Persephone could return to Earth for three months of the year. When she returned to Earth, she brought spring blooms with her thus becoming known as the Goddess of the spring.

I love spring and the first signs of the bluebells and daffodils every year is that annual reminder that we can survive anything. Despite the cold and the inevitable death that winter brings, the daffodil always blooms.

In the winter of 2019, I felt little hope and hit the notorious *rock bottom*. I had experienced domestic abuse and after a violent assault, I struggled with my mental health and suffered emotional and psychological burnout which resulted in a breakdown. 2020 was a year of growth for me and it was the spring that brought me new hope. As we all coped with the extending lockdowns there was a lone daffodil growing in my garden. I watched it bloom and on our daily walks it was the beauty of the daffodils that made me smile and Emilie rescued two broken daffodils to bring home. These sat together in a vase on my kitchen windowsill. We called them the *Mama and Baba daffodils* - that was one of the true joys of lockdown, I had time to just be, to enjoy the moment and see the positive around me after what had felt like a lifetime of darkness.

As a lover of writing and past blogger I reignited my blog calling myself *Blooming Daffodils*. I was celebrating the rebirth I felt after leaving the abusive relationship and starting the new phase in my life. This then became my business name as I started out as a mindfulness coach. The metaphor of 'blooming' has stayed with me and I will always cherish the fact that daffodils bloom every spring in spite of the cold and iciness that the ground has suffered during the winter.

As I began my journey of rebirth post-breakdown, I embodied that feeling of being the blooming daffodil. But as I carried on my healing journey I knew that I had done far more than grow. I had been reignited, I was the phoenix that had risen from the flames of abuse and depression, and I wanted to start a movement.

Mamas Ignited was born.

Imagine my delight when researching possible links between fire and blooming flowers that I discovered the origins of a *bloomery* – the traditional name for the process where rock was smelted to find the metal ore. What was even more staggering, and when the symbol of Fire became cemented as part of my brand, was when I discovered that the *bloom* is the name for the precious metal that has been smelted.

Like the *bloom* we are often put under immense pressure, feel intense heat and pain, yet we can survive and return strong and powerful like metal. To be strong, you first have to smelt and be moulded and then your *bloom* can be stronger than ever before. So like all precious metals, we, as women, often have to go through a lot of pain and pressure before we can be the *bloom*.

The name *Blooming Daffodils* had to go, but Persephone the Goddess of Spring is still very much at the heart of what *Mamas Ignited* represents. She fought her way back from the grip of Hades and the return of the spring blooms gives us hope that no matter the depths of icy pain and despair that we may endure, with time the sun will melt the icy ground and new life will return.

As a mindset and empowerment coach, I help women to tap into their story and be able to speak from the scar not the wound using it to ignite their business impact. I have had my share of adversity and know how hard it can be to stop listening to your inner critic, voice of doom and the tight grip of imposter syndrome and anxiety and the fear of judgement or failure.

The most pivotal moment of my growth was when I attended a vision board session just before lockdown. I was living in a vortex of doom at the time and looking back now I can see that I had a very fixed mindset as opposed to the growth mindset that I have now.

I couldn't see any positivity in my life but listening to Happiness coach and Author, Toni Mackenzie speak about how she overcame adversity it made me realise that I had the power within me to make a change. I decided there and then that '*positivity was my new mantra*'. Now as a Positive Psychology coach I can look back and see that I was using my positive thinking to broaden and build positive pathways and it is proven through the science of Positive Psychology that having a growth mindset and being high in hope allows people to take on goals and challenges that cultivates positive emotions, and positive self-talk. This is what happened – the more positive I became the more things began to change for the better.

Even though we are all at times struggling with life and adversity we are in control of how we think. In fact, it is reported through Positive Psychology studies that we all have a 40% opportunity to control our own happiness. Lyubomirsky's happiness pie chart says that 50% of our intrinsic happiness comes from Genetics, 10% is determined by life circumstances therefore meaning that 40% is down to our intentional activities. Making the choice to actively be more positive was life changing and was the beginning of my growth and testament to the resilience that I have.

Everything within my business is based on my own lived experience alongside my expertise and accreditations in mindfulness, mindset, coaching and teaching experience. I had such a story to share and I shared my story this year in my Number One bestselling book, *Mamas Ignited: Stop Ironing, Start living*. I know that if it's possible for me, then anyone who has suffered trauma or abuse of any kind, can heal and grow and as I was writing my own story I had what some may describe as a *'calling'* to help other women share theirs.

No one should be trapped by their past, and there's no shame in calling yourself a survivor. We've all experienced life's hard knocks in one way or another but they can be a springboard for a healthy, whole future, rather than a cycle of shame and despair.

I use the analogy that 'an ironing board is a surfboard that gave up on its dreams and got a boring job.' For years I felt that I was the *ironing board* and although I loved teaching, I wasn't living my purpose. As an English teacher I felt that I was living up to the saying, *'Those who can do, those who can't... teach.'* Creating *Mamas Ignited* I am a living example of how it is never too late to reach for your dreams. My dream was to be a published author. I am surfing to success showing other mamas that they can be more, do more and have more... and that never involves more ironing!

RISING THROUGH RESILIENCE

One thing that all of the women who have contributed to this book have in common is resilience. Life sends us unexpected horrors at times and the only thing we can do is carry on. Being resilient is often not on purpose, it is something that we find when we have no other choice.

Resilient people are strong enough to adapt and change... and we can't despair if we feel like that's an uncomfortable place to be. It comes with experience. I often think of the palm tree - able to bend in the storms, but rarely uprooted. You may feel like that today, but don't be troubled. The storm makes you stronger!

Resilient people know who they are and accept themselves, both the good and the bad.

Resilient people have a strong support network; family, friends, peers, work colleagues. We don't need an army of support, just those significant individuals we can turn to when life gets rough or the waves feel too strong to navigate.

Resilient people are honest with themselves and others. They don't sweep things under the carpet and pretend their way through life. I've learned that if you don't deal with something, it will eventually deal with you.

As a Positive Psychology coach - Growth theory can be applied to resilience. Having a growth mindset means that you focus on the journey of experiencing, giving things a go, failing and learning until you succeed. Sometimes this is unintentional when going through trauma but people with resilience view life events as opportunities to grow. Failures are only setbacks and opportunities for improvement and learning. People with a growth mindset take charge of their success and the process of attaining it and maintaining it and as such show great resilience. You will see what I mean when you read the next eight chapters and the growth that each of these women have shown and in doing so how they found the positive and ability to live a fully ignited life.

These women also show courage. This is the ability to do something that frightens you and show strength in the face of pain or grief. Resilience is the all-round mental, emotional, and spiritual capacity to recover and overcome from difficulties. Courage and resilience together is what makes us *rise* from any adversity. They show strength of character and a need for grit but we all have the potential to tap into when needed.

SHE IS IGNITED

Resilience is like a muscle that can be strengthened and is there when we need it most. In 2019, I faced an epic eight-month long family court battle which pushed me to breaking point and in December 2019 I was reached an all-time low. I was in a very dark place mentally and subsequently suffered emotional and psychological burnout. My mental health declined and I hit rock bottom. I was signed off work and took the first steps towards recovery – I had an occupational health referral and talking therapy, which was incredible. As well as healing, it was also very forward thinking and positive and I realised in these sessions that I didn't need to be a teacher for the rest of my life… which was an assumption that I had made. Alongside this, I was recommended to try Relax Kids for my daughter who was also suffering with symptoms of PTSD and anxiety. We had a mindfulness session and it changed both our lives. We experienced the incredible power in dedicating time to be mindful, close and together.

Following that trauma, in 2020 I trained in mindfulness and relaxation coaching and during the pandemic began to deliver much needed family well-being classes in my local area and on zoom. It was at this point that I realised, in most cases the mums also needed support. I started running Relax Mums' courses and this was the beginning of *Mamas Ignited*. My all-time low was a catalyst for the some of the best decisions I've ever made and from the ashes I was ignited. I now work with women in group programmes and one-to-one as a mindset and empowerment coach and feel inspired every day in the work that I do.

To finish before I hand over to the first author, I would like to share with you my SPARKS system. I would also like to offer you a free SPARKS Masterclass here https:// mamasignited.co.uk/free-masterclass/.

SPARKS is my mindset and well-being system linked to positive psychology coaching. You are capable of anything; you are resilient and you can ignite your spark but here are a few tips from me.

STRENGTH - Celebrate your own strengths and be clear on your values. My key strength is 'Humour' and I know that this is one of the ways that I am so resilient as I can use my humour and bring joy to difficult situations.

POSITIVITY - Positive self-talk. Don't keep looping that same old junk. Set a different mental course, write things down if you need to, and then look at yourself every day and talk through the positives and affirmations. *'I am strong, I am calm.'*

ACCOMPLISHMENT - Reflect on your own life lessons, celebrations and move forward. There are things you may have done differently. Celebrate your awesomeness and learn from any mistakes. The great news is, that tomorrow is a new day and you can choose to learn from the past and start afresh! Grit is needed to accomplish things in life, Passion + Perseverance = grit. This makes you more resilient.

REFRAME – Look at the things that have happened 'for' you and re-tell the story to show what you have learned. Also, forgive yourself! 9/10 times the trauma is not your fault but many of us torment ourselves with what ifs: *what if I'd said no/spoken up sooner not gone out with him/left at the first sign...* None of these things are your fault. Reframe the story.

KINDNESS -Accept that making mistakes is a fact of life and you're not perfect! Take the pressure off and be kind to yourself. Take time to 'just be' and restore your mind through breathing, visualisation and activities that help to keep you in the moment.

SUPPORT – Look at the people that you are surrounding yourself with. Belonging a human need, so make sure that you show gratitude to the people by your side and remember that *Empowered people empower people!*

PROJECT COLLABORATOR BIO

LOUISA HERRIDGE

Louisa is the number one best-selling author of *Mamas Ignited: Stop Ironing, Start Living*, speaker and mindset and positive psychology coach. She has risen from the ashes of abuse and trauma; reborn in flames as the blazing leader of the *Mamas Ignited* movement, showing all mums that there can be more than the 2.4 and dreams are there for the taking.

Louisa, 42 from Warrington, is an entrepreneurial solo mum who has overcome domestic violence and debt and lived with chronic pain which led to depression and major back surgery. In the last two years, due to a violent assault at the hands of her ex-partner, she is healing from complex trauma and experienced emotional and psychological burnout, before finding and creating a new path in life whilst healing herself and young daughter too.

Following 20 years in leadership, coaching and teaching English, Louisa is now on a mission to encourage all women to believe in themselves, to ignite their spark to BE more, DO more and HAVE more. Louisa combines her tools for mindset, mindfulness and positive psychology to motivate and inspire women to create and build their own dream lives whether that be through building personal confidence or creating impact in business.

Louisa's previous publications include *Stop Ironing, Start Living* that hit 7 Amazon Number One on release in February 2022. Her first publication was as a Number One best-selling co-author in the collaboration *'Pride - Motivation and Inspiration for women juggling motherhood and business.'* and made waves with her solo debut *'Time to Ignite - the five-step mindfulness system'* in 2021.

She leads a range of workshops, courses and collaborative projects alongside her one-to-one coaching packages. She works with women wanting to ignite their spark and entrepreneurs to ignite their impact in business.

Louisa is a freelance writer with Chocolate PR and proof-reader with Authors & Co and in November 2022 will launch the second instalment *From the Ashes; She is Ignited.*

Louisa is well known for her fun-loving personality and lives out her mission statement... *An Ironing board is a surfboard that gave up on its dreams and got a boring job... don't be an ironing board!*

www.mamasignited.co.uk

www.facebook.com/mamasignited

www.instagram.com/mamasignited

www.linkedin.com/in/mamasignited

Buy a copy of *Mamas Ignited: Stop Ironing, Start Living*

1

BUY THE SHOES

AMY TURNER

*O*ne minute. Sixty seconds. That's it.

Have you really thought how long one minute can feel like? Waiting for your lunch to heat up in the microwave, waiting for the kettle to boil, running on a treadmill! That minute can seem like forever.

As I plunged through the ice-cold blue sky from 15,000 feet strapped to a total stranger who has entirely responsible for pulling the cord on our parachute, that was the best and quickest minute of my life!

I've never felt so alive (ironic considering I was hurtling towards the ground 120mph). I left the weight of the world in that tiny plane, so high I could see the curvature of the earth and launched myself out the door. Parachute up and gently drifting down to the lush, green carpeted ground I contemplated that life was different now, very different and I loved that thought.

It's taken me until my forties and a life changing disease to get there but here I am alive and ignited. So whilst you've got the time and energy, it seems sensible for you to do the same.

Once upon a time though, whilst I thought I was successfully smashing my career; I was in fact demolishing my life. Bit by bit until eventually I crumbled.

As a successful Assistant Principal in a high school, I had climbed the career ladder rapidly and done well. Moving from teacher to the dizzy heights of senior leader, I was happy and felt accomplished - or so I thought.

Life B.C (before children) was very different, and I could dip in and out work at my leisure, but I suppose looking back I never realised the number of hours I was unconsciously clocking up: marking exam papers in my pyjamas on a Sunday morning, writing university statements for college students over the Christmas holidays so they were in for the January deadline.

God knows what teachers would earn in overtime if we got it.

But once I became a mum, the windows of opportunity to operate like this diminished and my working day began to look, well, ridiculous. From the outside however, it looked like I had it all - a nice home, a nice car, a great family, a great career, fabulous friends. I was blissfully ignorant to the fact that I was killing myself.

Mistaking unproductive late nights for being a hard worker, powering through the crippling fatigue, I kept calm and carried on. There's an adage about a frog that when put into a pan of boiling water, it will jump straight out, however when placed into a pan of cold water which is gradually heated up, it will go into a stupor and ignorantly sit there until it is boiled to death. My pot was heating up and I didn't even realise.

At my worst, when my husband was working abroad, I'd come home from a ten-hour day, run errands, deal with family life, put my daughter to bed and then eventually begin the work I needed to do just to stay treading water in my job. Dinner would be a bag of crisps that I could quickly grab, washed down with a glass of rioja to help me relax. I'd work until the small hours, scheduling in a power nap around 11pm.

Having terrible FOMO (fear of missing out) I'd also somehow squeeze in a busy social life. I wore the term *hard-working* like a badge of honour.

Crazy though it sounds in hindsight, I didn't feel I could say I wasn't coping. As one of a few females in a male heavy management environment which had been through endless restructures, proving myself and my worth was my only choice and didn't matter how I achieved this. Women can have it all right? Or can we? Why do we even need to? I felt I couldn't show any chinks in my armour, but I was fooling myself. I already had a bad case of imposter syndrome, so I kept going.

I mistook 'self-care' for the odd bath or expensive spa day which didn't have any long-term benefits to my mental and physical health. I've since realised that this is not the definition of this new phenomenon of 'self-care' but rather the little things found in the small moments of life like ten minutes of meditation, sitting on my bed quietly or even just taking a breath and relaxing my tense jaw and shoulders when I'm feeling overwhelmed and stressed.

This period of self-sabotage lasted some time, but I was so caught up in the cycle, I couldn't really see what was happening, let alone make any changes. I was sure this was what it's like *at the top*.

I suppose looking back I used work to deal with life, throwing myself into it at every opportunity. I may have created wealth, but I certainly hadn't created health. I was tired, I was miserable but papered over the cracks with crazy nights out, holidays or shopping without dealing with the root of my problems.

When we use escapisms, they can only last for so long. Yet perversely, I still enjoyed work. I've always been a naturally cheery person and you wouldn't have known from the outside - hell I didn't even know!

But I was tired, I was also tired because I wasn't doing much that fed my soul. Nothing was setting me on fire, nothing was nourishing me and that too can make a person really miserable. I wasn't aligned, I was vibrating at a low frequency – my spirituality diminishing. I was in my ego not my heart.

I actually feel kind of embarrassed now, looking back on how much of my identity was being an Assistant Principal. I cringe at the fact that I'd often lead with this in conversation. I suppose I enjoyed the power, the money and was proud of where I'd got to in my career.

As time went on, cracks started to show. I recall sitting in a meeting, a session that was held every week that I helped chair. I felt oppressed. Oppressed and suddenly overwhelmed. As I sat there listening to the BS being bantered about the room, I felt engulfed with rage and then panic. I needed to get out. I whispered to my colleague that I had to get out. Thinking I was unwell, he asked if I was ok. *'I just need to leave'* I told him as he saw my usual unflappable face become panic stricken and registered something was wrong. And with that I marched out. My heels sounding deafeningly loud as I ran down the stairs leaving a room full of confused people.

Not long after, the head came to see me. Not about my impromptu exit from the meeting but to discuss another member of staff. Then it happened. That frog I previously mentioned suddenly realised this was no jacuzzi and hopped out.

'I can't do this' I blurted out mid conversation. *'I can't do this anymore. This isn't what I want'*. Have you ever heard yourself

speaking and it's almost like an out of body experience? Like you're listening to what's coming out of your mouth but it's not you who is saying the words. Almost as if you're being divinely guided.

There I was, twenty years into my career saying f**k it. Was I mad? Maybe. Was I scared? No. In fact it felt beautifully liberating. There's something so refreshing in speaking a truth.

Though I'd flirted with various other career ideas, I definitely hadn't thought this move through. Shit.

However, once I'd taken that first step, I felt present. I felt alive. It's scary to take an action with no attachment to outcome, but it's often the only way if you truly want to make a change. I had to trust the process, and this is exactly what I did.

I'd always enjoyed languages and teaching had always been (and always will) be my passion. When I was much younger and in the sixth form, I worked for a wonderful lady who had a children's language school. I taught French almost every evening between my studies to the tinniest of tots. To be fair, it didn't feel like work - not like the grim Saturday job I had in retail. I was amazed at their sponge – like brains, soaking up language and culture through song and play. This is what I wanted. My own language school, to be my own boss, to find my passion for teaching again. So, I set about making this happen.

Now, here dear reader, you may raise an eyebrow of disbelief, but my first business venture came to me in what I can only call an epiphany dream. It was a *'sit upright in disbelief and excitement'* moment in the middle of the night. Maybe I just had more clarity, maybe my mind was freed from its stresses to be creative again. Maybe it was divine intervention. Who knows? But it was enough to light my fire.

So I said goodbye to my management responsibilities, went part time and *Lingo Language School* was born. If you're thinking *well that sounds easy enough*, it wasn't so straightforward. For a start, I took the mother of all pay cuts. Not so easy to do when you have a family and a mortgage and enjoy the feeling of being able to 'see it, want it, buy it'. But did I appreciate this? Not always. Did it make me happy? No.

I threw my energy into trusting the process. In the same way that we drive at night down an unfamiliar road, at night, we can't see the road in the dark, but we trust ourselves it is there.

Little did I know that it was a little cluster of rapidly multiplying cancer cells that would give me the ultimate push to make me change my ways.

Monday morning and the G.U.M clinic was packed wall to wall with all manner of people. Predominantly male millennials in tracksuits, waiting patiently to see if they'd brought home more than a phone number on Saturday night.

As I surveyed the room trying to avoid eye contact, my name was called. In the sterile room I sat on the cold metal chair and confessed like a naughty child that I'd skipped my smear tests. Not one, but several which yes, accumulated to years. I wasn't scared or prudish. But I was busy. That seems so feeble as I write it but as the letters came through the door, I'd think *'yep, I must do that' but I've got x,y and z.to do'* or *'Oh I must call about my screening'*. But I never did. I did everything but that.

I was experiencing some symptoms though that in my heart of hearts, I knew weren't right. For too long I'd passed them off as other things. Irregular bleeding – must be approaching the menopause (I was 44 after all). Aches and pains in my pelvic bones – must be all those squats in the gym or maybe my body just wasn't the same after having a baby. You can't lug something the size of a watermelon around for three quarters of a year and go unscathed right?

Tiredness and fatigue were overwhelming, but I was busy and a mum. Find me a mum to a three-year-old that isn't tired. I certainly wouldn't have bothered my doctor with any of those things but as they persisted and intensified something told me to get checked. Much as I have the utmost praise for our wonderful NHS, getting a doctor's appointment must have lower odds than landing your chosen number and colour on a roulette wheel hence me taking myself off to the clinic.

'Right, get on that table now' said the nurse as she prepped my nether regions. Leave your dignity at the door I thought. She asked me a series of questions. *'In the past two weeks, have you had vaginal, oral or anal sex?'* *'Do I win a prize if I say yes to all three'* I joked. She didn't laugh. I'd read about a GP surgery somewhere that had a picture of George Clooney on the celling where patients had their smear tests to make the process slightly more 'comfortable' - I'd be delusional saying enjoyable. Whilst she set to work with her chilly speculum (could have warmed it up first hon) I looked up for George's kind brown eyes only to be met with the sight of a dead fly in a very unflattering strip light.

Fast forward two weeks and I'm back again, legs akimbo whilst I had a laser procedure to remove some cells which were on the turn. That makes it sound like some old fruit in your fridge. A biopsy was taken as a routine, and I was told they'd contact me in about two weeks with the result. When I got a phone call at my desk two days later, I knew things had just gone up a gear.

Back at work, a colleague tried to reassure me. *'Maybe they just want to talk to you about not getting checked out sooner'*. Yeah right, as if the NHS have got time to sit and have a chat and give me a wee ticking off for my poor organisational skills.

May 4th. May the 'fourth' be with you and all that. A day that will be etched on my memory forever. Have you ever fallen, or watched someone fall over and it felt like it was happening in slow motion? Words came in fragments even though I was listening intently. *'Stage 1b.' 'Cervical cancer.' 'Radical hysterectomy.' 'Radiotherapy.'*

As my world fell off its axis, I felt strangely numb. Then I spotted the young nurse sat slightly behind the consultant taking notes, her eyes brimming with tears. Maybe she was moved as I was young or had a beautiful little three-year-old girl waiting for me at nursey or maybe she was just beaten down by the sheer number of ladies she saw daily, receive this news. Shit just got real.

I wandered out into the hospital concourse clutching my Macmillan information booklets showing smiling ladies in head scarves. I called my best friend. *'You'd better sit down'* I said, and we sobbed and sobbed. I messaged a senior colleague at school. Once she'd said how sad/sorry she was, she suggested I didn't come back in that afternoon. Erm, as if. Sure, I'll just put my happy head on like Worzel Gummidge and crack on with another fun packed, educational hour teaching how to order food in a Spanish café to a class of naughty year 8 kids. Let me think that one over.

What I did was quite bizarre. Well to some people. A gorgeous new boutique had just opened in town, and I'd got a stunning dress for an upcoming christening reserved there until the end of the day. So I dried my eyes, put my metaphorical big girl knickers on and went to collect it from the very glamorous lady who owned it. This beautiful lady turned out to be even more beautiful on the inside and became one of my best of friends. She ended up being one of my 'go to' people on this journey and beyond.

There's one thing about having cancer, it sorts out the wheat from the chaff in terms of friends. I was fortunate to have a strong tribe around me. Ones who texted and called every single day, ones who sent things to cheer me up, one who sat by my hospital bed whilst I had a blood transfusion for hours even though it was her boyfriend's birthday, one who spent their days off sat with me at radiotherapy appointments. But then there are ones who move away, who maybe don't know what to say, so say nothing. If I can ask one thing of you when you hear bad news like a cancer diagnosis of a friend or loved one and you don't know what to say, say that – *'I don't know what to say.'* Anything is better than nothing - believe me. Cancer can be a **VERY** lonely place.

So new dress in hand, I saw that Nando's looked quiet and optimistically went in to get lunch. I couldn't eat. Who was I kidding. I felt choked. The scraps I managed tasted salty mixed with my tears, but the cold glass of rosé sure went down well. I haven't got time to be sick I thought. Typical. Survival mode <u>on</u>.

As it happens this was just the beginning and like life so often does, it threw me a few more curve balls. My cancer had spread to my lymph nodes. The lymph nodes have a very important job. They are like our very own filter system, getting rid of all the crap in our bodies like bacteria and viruses that cause illness. So the thing in my body that stops me being ill is ill. Right.

This called for drastic action and my treatment plan was changed to a very heady cocktail of daily radiotherapy, chemotherapy and brachytherapy. If you've never heard of the latter ladies, look it up. You'll never miss a smear test again. Guaranteed.

I was warned this wasn't going to be easy, that the thing that would ultimately better would make me sick and boy they were right. Time for those big girl knickers.

I feel like I speak in cliches since my diagnosis but when you have a brush with mortality, it changes you.

My change wasn't instant though. In my head I thought *'I don't have time to be ill.'* I'd launched my company the previous month. It was going well. I didn't want time off from either job. I was bothered about my looks. I didn't want to lose my hair. Spoiler alert: I didn't. Hooray you say! Well instead I lost my hearing and ended up with a hearing aid and was flung into early menopause. You can't win them all right?

Much as I wanted to fight this hideous disease and retain an amount of 'normality' in life I still hadn't mastered the art of not giving a shit. I remember driving to the hospital for my radiotherapy session. By this time, I was way into my treatment and it was having some particularly hideous side effects: nausea, vomiting, incontinence and fatigue like I'll never be able to convey. Fatigue that sometimes stopped my legs working, that forced me to lie on the settee to play catch with my daughter as I just couldn't stand - her standing just outside the patio doors in the sun and me, inside, horizontal, holding back the nausea trying to be as normal as possible. The C word was one I didn't teach her. She didn't need to know and doesn't until the time is right.

So there I was, going for another dose of life saving treatment when I saw a coach leaving the school grounds where I worked. It was heading off on a school trip – a trip I should have been on, and it made me feel sad. I felt like I was missing out. I gave myself a shake. I was going to have lifesaving treatment and I wanted to be in work. Clearly that boiling frog I mentioned before still had a toe in the water.

This became evident when I decided just weeks out of treatment to return to work. The toxic blend of chemicals still swirling around my body doing their thing. I suppose I wanted to be 'normal' again – whatever normal was now. I looked ok - hair done, make up on, heels on, but on the inside I was reeling.

I was treated at face value: I looked fine, therefore I must be fine. So back I went, no system in place to support me. Little did they know that the caretaker had to carry my bags and mountains of books to the top floor of the building where I worked. This was a smack in the face for me and a huge wake up call.

I'd devoted my life to a place that quite frankly didn't really care. I was just a number, I wasn't indispensable, some of these people were just colleagues, not friends, it was *just a job!*

This life didn't serve me anymore and it was time for a change. I quit altogether and went full steam ahead with my company. Twenty years gone. A £50,000 plus pay cheque a year gone.

I'd never felt so alive. I trusted my higher self and knew it would be ok.

My friend's mum always said '*don't regret the things you've done; regret the things you didn't do*'. I had been existing for too long, it was time to start living.

The little things shouldn't matter, they aren't the things you whirl over in your mind when you're sat with a cannula in your hand pumping poison onto you. Whether I contributed well to a meeting or got a document in on time weren't the things that I thought long and hard about when I was lying awake at night in pain, instead I was mulling over funeral songs (Somewhere Over the Rainbow by Isarael Kamakawi-wo'ole if you're interested). Don't get me wrong, I'm not saying be careless but just 'care less' about things.

One of my last fun days out before the proverbial hit the fan was to the Grand National with my beautiful friend Stephanie. I'd bought some shoes, expensive shoes. These shoes were a thing of beauty with little wings on the back. If you know you know, a bit like the red soled ones. I had a huge row with my husband about the price of them. They were excessive I admit. I tried doing the 'these old things' trick but it didn't wash. Wracked with buyer's remorse I toyed with sending them back. I didn't and three weeks later I was being told I had a life changing illness. Suddenly a pair of shoes didn't even deserve any attention or energy. I kept them, I wore them, they looked FABULOUS. No regrets.

Speaking of fashion, when did stress become the new black? We seem to be constantly 'on' with little or no downtime. One cure I've found to being constantly 'on' is 'om' aka – a little yoga goes a long way and has become the best type of exercise for a menopausal lady like myself. Ah the menopause – I could write a whole chapter just on that. Mine was inflicted upon me as my poor little eggs are now fried from my radiation treatment. Cancer – the gift that keeps giving *eyerolling here*.

This constant state of being switched on leads up to a build of stress hormones. I'm no Doctor, but I'm pretty sure these hormones gave my cancer a helping hand to flourish.

Being a former self-confessed control freak then suddenly having zero control of life – my body doing what it wanted despite being young and healthy, a team of people making decisions about my body for me and all the other things that I suddenly couldn't do, was in retrospect a wonderful lesson.

I don't sweat the small stuff anymore or hold grudges. The only person holding grudges affects is you. It eats away at you like a hungry moth nibbling on a jumper. Just let the arseholes be arseholes. You'll be amazed how refreshing this feels. Nowadays I make like Elsa and 'let it go'.

I could be accused of wearing rose tinted specs but what's the point in lugging all those grievances around with you.

I'm not even mad at getting cancer. This horrible time has led to some pretty amazing things. One of my main focuses now is giving back and fundraising for the Clatterbridge Cancer Hospital that worked their magic on me. I've been on the radio, in the press, been guest speaker at charity dinners, taken part in charity fashion shows and have so far raised thousands of pounds doing crazy things like my parachute jump and an abseil of the Liverpool Cathedral (FYI it's huge).

No mud, no lotus, right? Oh yes, something else I did – got a tattoo of a lotus on my wrist just to give me a reminder of how far I've come.

Earlier I spoke about caring less. Much as I enjoy work and consider myself to be successful, I am less bothered about it. This is a difficult one to achieve. I remember reading in the fabulous book 'Shine" by Andy Cope and Gavin Oates about a spectrum of 'botherdness'. Swing too far one way and you risk experiencing no joy, no risks, no feeling of achievement as you simply don't care and apathy sneaks in. Swing the other way and suddenly you're consumed by work.

Teachers are especially guilty of this. Often, we view these kids as if they were our own. In *loco parentis*. If you're not careful it defines you and when that is taken away by illness or redundancy or whatever it may be, unless you have a strong sense of self besides the work version of you, you're going to feel pretty lost.

Do a good job, give it your best but remember it's exactly that – a job and there are many other facets to your beautiful, shiny self.

Gratitude has been a key factor in my healing too and how I go about life now. I haven't always been grateful. Sometimes when you're angry or sad it's hard to find that golden nugget of something to be grateful for.

I can recall a time a time during my treatment. I was having a really, really bad day. I felt very isolated despite having a good network of lovely people around me and was physically having a very shitty day – literally. I was vomiting, running to the toilet and generally feeling like a hostage in my own body. When I walked in from the hospital there was some post on the kitchen counter. One of the packages was from one of my best friends, it was a piece of cake. A piece of cake when I can't keep a sip of water in! Are you kidding me? Why doesn't she just visit me I thought? Screw the cake and call me and talk to me to help ease this loneliness I thought as I launched said cake down the kitchen.

Now I look back and realise that was actually a good deed that was coming from a good place. Maybe I should have picked the phone up. I should have been grateful for having such a lovely friend who was thinking of me. Gratitude is a great tool to reframe things. As it happens, the cake was really nice, and my friend is wonderful.

The pursuit of happiness is to some extent futile and moreover impossible, and some may find my next piece of advice a little morose but lowering our expectations can really help with our happiness. As a bit of a former people pleaser and overachiever I wasn't always on board with this concept. But all too often we have unrealistic expectations of people and measure their version of things against our own. Expectations can form such disappointment and only we have the power to control that. You have your thing and someone else has theirs.

In my opinion, no one cleans our house like I do. I'm right up there with Mrs Hinch, sprinkling Zoflora and white vinegar in my trail. This doesn't mean the job the others do is terrible, just the opposite and I'm super grateful to come home to a clean house. My expectations are unrealistically high. Simple. Some things just really aren't worth getting your knickers in a twist about. I was listening to Chris Evans on the radio, and he advised that before you get mad about something and launch an attack on someone, just think in your head, on a scale of one to five (one being of no or little significance and five being something super serious that needs addressing, something years down the line that will still make you bristle) just rate that problem and all too often if will come out as a one or two and disperse. Fact.

'You're an inspiration' is a something I get told a lot these days. It's nice to be told this but I'd disagree. Having had cancer does not make me an inspiration at all. If that was the case, anyone with an illness would be inspirational. Not that I'm playing Top Trumps with ailments, but there are plenty of folk out there dealing with much more than I had to. I suppose the way I handled myself during that time and the life I have carved out after it warrants a pat on the back.

Something I hope I have achieved through my work with Clatterbridge and wonderful charities like Jo's Trust, Shine and more recently a fabulous group called The C-list is to help raise awareness.

Firstly, the importance of keeping up to date with your smear tests or paying attention to any unusual symptoms. The amount of people who I have come across who have since booked in for this 5-minute lifesaving procedure is incredible. I guess we all think it will never happen to us.

My other passion is helping others. Whether that be through testimonials – often warts and all for others embarking on their cancer journey or guidance on how to support people. A recent YouTube video I made for the C-list spoke about being mindful of people looking ok but feeling ill and not judging a book by its cover. Even in remission when you think you should be clicking your heels and celebrating, it can be a scary time when your medical team steps away, and you have come out the other side of the process a totally different person.

Let's just be kind to each other, we are all ultimately, just walking each other home.

I wish it hadn't taken cancer to help me make the changes in my life that I have. Don't get me wrong, I'm still not there yet but I don't fear change anymore and have relinquished my need to control. Having had plenty of time hooked up to a chemo drip or lying in an MRI tube to think, I vowed I'd never live a vanilla life. I'd live it in full, glorious colour with an extra sprinkle of fabulous.

I won't end on a motivational quote, I'm really not a fan of them, especially that *'live, laugh, love'* one hung in many a room. But it is rather good advice. Do that. Lots of it. Oh, and buy the shoes...

ABOUT THE AUTHOR

AMY TURNER

Amy Turner, from Warrington is a French and Spanish teacher and the director of her own language school *Lingo Language School* based in and around the Warrington area.

After a short spell as cabin crew and twenty years teaching in a secondary school as an Assistant Principal, Amy established *Lingo Languages* which provides small group and private language tuition, PPA cover for schools, corporate language support, consultation work and bid writing. She now how has a better work life balance whilst still following her passion for teaching and language learning.

She is an avid fundraiser and has raised a considerable amount for the Clatterbridge Cancer Charity, which is very close to her heart after being treated there. She also works with other charities including Jo's Trust and the media to raise awareness of the importance of cervical screening. When she's not abseiling down a building or sky diving out of a plane to raise money, she enjoys yoga and is a qualified reiki practitioner.

This chapter is dedicated to mum and dad - the most selfless, kind parents anyone could ask for. To you I owe the world. Also, to my husband Colin for being so tolerant and supportive and my beautiful daughter Lola – I hope you inherit strength and kindness and live your life to its fullest just like mum. Finally, to my friend tribe - you know who you all are. Thanks to you all, I laughed a little harder and cried a little less.

Email: info@lingolanguages.co.uk

amyturner2211@gmail.com

2

THE SCIENCE OF HAPPINESS

FAYE EDWARDES

$\mathcal{W}$e can do hard things[1]

Life is hard. Life is supposed to be hard. But we seem to be under the impression that life was supposed to be easy, and then when it gets hard, we feel hard done by. And we also seem to be under the impression that the rest of the world have it easy, much easier than us, and then that's not fair. Because it is hard for us.

Life is hard.

We are humans. We have human emotions. Life was always supposed to be hard. But we are made to cope. We can either:

a)   take a deep breath, and embrace life in all its hard-ness.

or

b) moan, and get tired, and get bitter, because we don't want to do the hard. And then get more bitter because other people seem to have it better than us.

Both of those options are a choice.

Everyone goes through really tough times. Even though at the time, it can feel as though our tough time is tougher than everyone else's, it isn't. It is really important to understand that what we are going through is a difficult, but 'normal' part of life. Here are some of the things we all go through in the course of our lives:

Heartbreak

Serious illness

Pain

Bereavement

Betrayal

Financial issues

Disappointment

But, here is the part that is *the* most important. You are absolutely fully capable of doing the hard parts. You already have everything you need within you now. Trust yourself to be able to cope, to get through it. To get through it smiling, positive, strong, happy and together. You can even help other people through their hard times. You totally have all this within you right now.

The moment we change our perception of what life deals us, is the moment everything shifts. Your moment can be right now.

This is not 'your lot'.

This is not 'just your luck'.

This is not 'just typical'.

This is YOUR shot.

Take it.

WE BOUGHT A FOREST

I am so grateful for the experiences that life has given me. Some of them were absolutely shocking at the time. But now, age fifty-five, a mum of two wonderful children, and boss of a thriving, successful business, I know I have my difficult experiences to thank for enabling me to be where I am now.

For many years, I was very successful in my career, I had a fantastic quality of life, I had a huge circle of friends, and life was just generally good. I lived in London and truly lived, and loved, the life. In fact, I can't think of a better place to spend your twenties. The thing is, when you're successful, you don't really need to look within yourself. You have everything you want and need. You're respected professionally, you rock up and do your thing, everything is going great… until it isn't. I loved my job, I travelled all over the world, I worked in sustainability and I knew the work I was doing was shaping the future of the planet. Awesome, right?

I genuinely didn't know what personal growth was - why would I? I'd had no need to find out. I had actually been to a couple of guided meditation sessions in Covent Garden - meeting your inner child kind of thing. I absolutely loved them, but had no desire to think about them any further than being a fun night out. I had also read Shakti Gawain 'Creative Visualisation' when I was about 18. I thought it was a bit of fun, and so didn't think about it again for many (many) years.

When the children were three and four, we made a huge decision and moved to Cornwall and bought a forest. It was utter paradise. Suddenly, I'd gone from concrete, pavements, traffic and noise, to peace, tranquility, beauty and nature. It was absolute bliss.

I had never run a business before. I had done property renovations with my husband, but never actually run a client facing business. I loved it. But it was full on. With no knowledge of there being any other way, I was definitely working IN the business, rather than ON the business. At that beginning time, my days were spent washing bed linen, pulling up brambles, ordering cleaning products, setting up a website, teaching myself the booking system and many other things. It was varied but I quickly had to learn how to prioritise the income generating tasks, because the day-to-day maintenance and admin would quite simply - never stop!

We had refinanced another property to be able to purchase Tresarran (the forest) - a perfectly normal property strategy. There is always risk in these kind of things but I had worked with my broker for a long time and trusted his judgment. Everything seemed to be moving along as expected and we were waiting for the refinance to come through so we could settle the original borrowing. However, on one fateful day, while I was watching my children play on a playground by the most beautiful lake, I took the phone call that was going to change everything. The broker called to break the news that the finance offer had been withdrawn without any possibility of it being reinstated. I learnt that due to an admin error on the Land Registry, the financing could not be approved. I was suddenly facing the very real prospect of losing over half a million pounds. I was floored.

FROM THE GROUND UP

Life was starting to swirl around me. I was completely lost. I couldn't speak to my friends, my sisters or anyone for that matter. I was still functioning. I was still doing the school run, I was still running the business. In fact, looking back, I am so grateful to the school run during that period. It gave my life structure and meaning and purpose, and it gave me a reason to wash my hair, and put mascara on. However, I was absolutely flailing on the inside. My head was filled with thoughts of *'I'm so broken, I have failed everyone, I am worthless'*.

I now know, that so many other people feel those feelings too. But at the time, I thought I was the only person in the world who felt like that. So, if you ever have those thoughts, please know that it is not just you. So many of us have moments like that when we doubt everything, and we doubt ourselves, and we doubt the world around us. Having come out the other side, I can tell you now that it is most likely to be the start of the most amazing journey that you have ever been on. But I had no one there to tell me that. I felt as though I was losing control of everything, and I most certainly was not coping.

A SOUND BATH? WHAT'S THAT?

I had an invitation from a friend to go to a sound bath. A sound bath? What the hell is that? I had no idea what to expect, but something told me that I had to go. I got my yoga mats, and my blanket, and slightly nervous and hesitant, drove us to a wonderful house in Cornwall and was met by the most angelic-looking silver haired lady. I was nervous, and spent so much time wondering if I might do everything wrong, or if everyone else would realise that it was my first one. I needn't have worried. It was an unbelievable experience.

There were about twenty of us in a dark cosy room laying on blankets and fluffy cushions. A wonderful skinny man with long silver hair emerged. He introduced himself as Sika, from New Zealand. He was clearly very famous to everyone else in the room, and the buzz of excitement was palpable. We all laid down, and the journey began. I say journey, because it was a journey, the like of which I had never been on before. Using didgeridoos, chimes, windpipes and skin drums, Sika took us all on this roller coaster of emotions. He used the sounds and vibrations to lift us up, and then drop us as we fell through the air of our own imagination. I felt myself falling and falling deeper into myself, it was as though I was being swallowed by a deep dark hole and swirled around in every direction. I didn't really know what was happening, and tears were streaming down my face and I could feel my whole body wracked with sobs. My head was full of thoughts. It was so so full. The thoughts were coming so fast I could barely keep up with them. My thoughts were all about how awful I was, how broken I was, how I drank too much, what a bad person I was, how disorganised I was, how I should be so much better at life, how fat I was, how grumpy I was. It was truly awful. I felt absolutely broken and ashamed of what a failure I had become.

We had been given a paper and pen and I started to write all of these feelings of self-hatred and loathing onto the piece of paper. I couldn't write fast enough. I could feel the waves of shame ebb through me as I was writing and it made me cry more and more. Then, once the writing had stopped, I felt so embarrassed to be so emotional. The other people were wandering around laughing and smiling, and there was I, tear stained and a wreck.

I went to the loo to clean myself up, and bumped into my friend, Tina. I remember so clearly telling her that my heart hurt. My poor aching heart. I was actually worried that there was something physiologically wrong with my heart and that this was some kind of message that I needed to get to a doctor. I had the piece of paper covered in my scribbles of self-loathing in the back pocket of my jeans. I remember thinking that I had to copy it out neatly when I got home.

Over the next few days, I felt that piece of paper burning a hole in my back pocket, taunting me that it was there. I had every intention of taking it out and writing it all up into my notebook. I know it was there and was busy with life, and work, and children. I didn't quite find the time to get it out and have a read through it. One morning, I emptied the tumble dryer and found it was full of bits of paper. Immediately, I was devastated. It was gone. I had meant to have a copy of it and read through it again. Then I realised, why would I want to read through it again? Those words had been so painful, and so heavy and harsh. I began to berate myself again, *'I'm so stupid, why didn't I check my pockets before I put the wash on? I'm a bad person, a rubbish mum, I'm terrible at everything…'.*

Then, in an instant, I felt a huge sense of release. I could feel the weight of those words literally lift and leave my body. I felt lighter, un-weighted and as if something I had been carrying was no longer a worry anymore. I had not meant to wash and dry that piece of paper that was full of my own hateful scribbling, but by doing so, I had released all of those feelings. They were gone. I didn't have to feel those things about myself anymore. There didn't need to be anymore self-hate. Instead, I realised, there needed to be self-love.

HEALING

That was my first real sense of the power of healing. I'm sure that the wonderful Sika had no idea of the profound affect that sound bath had on me, and my future. And if I ever told him, he'd probably say *'ah bless'*, because he could never know how powerful that was.

I don't think I even realised at the time that I had experienced healing. I just knew that I had had an almighty shift and that I needed more, and I wanted to know how to facilitate that happening. I was searching for the tools I needed to continue the journey of getting to know myself better.

I joined numerous female entrepreneur groups and they were a fantastic source of information. I did an incredible Sound Goddess course and became a qualified sound therapist. I did reiki practitioner training, I became a qualified meditation leader. I started walking from six to seven am each morning. I was absolutely buzzing from all of these new parts of my life and how they worked together, and how they worked *for* me. I knew now that healing was possible. I don't think I had ever thought about it properly before this point, and if anything, I had been sceptical that it was a real thing at all.

HOW TO WAKE UP SMILING

I suddenly found that I was waking up smiling every single day. I had stopped drinking alcohol and that made a huge difference to the way I felt in the mornings, but I also had a golden energy that was always pulsing away within me.

I had developed a little routine where I started the day by thinking of three things that I was grateful for as soon as I got out of bed. It made me laugh every day because every day, one of the things was always tea. Tea is amazing! I had also listened to (Audible is my best friend), Mel Robbins book, *'The 5 second rule'* - and that was a huge help. It made me leap out of bed each morning and want to totally embrace the day. I also listened to *'You can heal your life'* by Louise Hay, and suddenly, I realised that my future was in my hands. That was a ground breaking moment for me. I thought hugely successful people had something different from me, that they were literally better in some way! That they had huge good luck, and that their amazing lifestyles just fell conveniently into their laps. Yet, here I was, just turned forty, a mum of two, and finally realising that this life was *mine* for the taking. No one else's...just mine. And there was only me that could make it amazing too.

I then began researching successful people. I wanted to know, *'what did they have in common?'*. I absorbed their stories as though they were life blood and started to see trends in what they were doing. I read, listened to and watched, as many inspirational people as I could and had my next huge breakthrough - being happy is totally and utterly, one hundred per cent in our control. Life does not have to happen *to* us, we make our own lives happen *for* us.

THE SCIENCE OF HAPPINESS

I genuinely felt as though I had found the secret to life itself (and yes, I did read *The Secret*). I have a very logical mind, and always wanted to see scientific proof of theories to evidence them. If happiness was a science, didn't we all have the power to apply the principles to our lives?

People often ask me now, *'why did you start the Positive Living Movement? You're a successful property investor.'* I can understand their question. I have sometimes asked myself the same question.

I was walking in the woods one day, as I often do. It was just me and the dog, early in the morning. This early walk had become part of my daily routine, and honestly, I never wanted to get out of bed at 5am when my alarm went off. But there was never a day when I wasn't so utterly pleased that I had.

On that particular day, I was listening to an audiobook as I usually did, and I couldn't concentrate on the words. I remember really clearly, I was a bit cross with myself as I kept having to rewind the book as I had been drifting away and missing parts of the story. The sun was just starting to glint through the trees, in that beautiful way it does in the forest, and I can still hear the sounds of the birds and the smell of the pine trees, exactly as it was that morning.

In the end, I paused the audiobook because I realised I needed to think without distraction. Almost immediately, I was full of ideas. It was almost as though I hadn't actually thought of them myself. The ideas just kept flowing and by the end of the walk, I had formed the *Positive Living Movement*. It was a fully formed idea and I could see how this movement could reach millions of people and share the techniques and exercises that could help them change their loves too.

I had heard of 'channelling' before, but I don't think I would have really believe it existed until I experienced it myself. The thing is, we all have the power to channel, and to receive ideas passively. Have you ever had a passing thought about something, and brushed it off as your crazy brain having silly ideas? If you have, then don't! Our subconscious has some truly powerful messages for us. It is sending our conscious mind messages and ideas all the time. Yet, we are told, by society, not to get too carried away with our thoughts, not to get too big for our boots and not to have ideas above our station - so we learn to ignore these hugely powerful and fundamentally important thoughts in order to keep ourselves small.

Do me a favour, please don't ever feel the need to keep yourself small.

I know now that my mission, my purpose, my meaning is to share this with as many people as possible so they can take control of their lives too. I am so fortunate that my accomplishment is satisfied in my success in the property industry, but my calling is so much greater than that. I now speak to schools, online communities, young women and corporates about how they can sustainably apply the principles of the science of happiness to change their outlook, their opportunities and most importantly, their mindset.

I came across a book called *'Now is Your Chance'* by a wonderful woman, Niyc Pidgeon. I devoured this book, and I totally resonated with everything she said, but also, I could identify with her. She was a girl from the north of England with a mission and a message, and that was to serve others by sharing the findings of positive psychology. What made this book so special, was that all of the techniques were backed up by scientific studies. It was literally proven that by following these steps, you could be happier. It was also so easy to read, it felt as though I was listening to a friend. When I read the simple things that we can all do each day to improve our moods and our outlook, it all felt so possible, so achievable.

I began studying positive psychology, which is essentially, the science of well-being. From the start, I felt as though I had found my *'thing'*. It was as though someone had been reading my mind. All the things that I had been doing in my daily life, were outlined in this science. One of the best explanations of positive psychology is this. Whereas psychology often focuses on what's 'wrong' with you and tries to fix it, positive psychology focuses on what you're amazing at, and how to make the most of that in your life, work, business, relationships, health, family - everything!

So many of us spend our whole lives berating ourselves for the things we are not good at. This forms a pattern of self-loathing that then becomes the way we think about ourselves and feel about ourselves. There are so many things we think we should be 'better' at (in comparison with other people), when in actual fact, we all have our zone of genius. We don't even need to worry about the things that we are not perfect at, because, guess what, no one is perfect at everything.

Have you ever thought any of these things?

I'm disorganised

I'm always late

I'm too loud

I'm no good with money

I don't like crowds of people

I don't like change

I'm too much

I'm not enough

I'm not good enough

I'm too big

I'm too small

I'm oversensitive

I'm unfit

I don't know how to deal with people

Yes! I thought they might. Some will resonate and some won't. All that proves is that we are all different. Each and every one of us has our own strengths and our own zones of genius. They will never all be the same and we can never be amazing at everything - no matter how much it may seem that some people are! What we need to focus on, is what we are amazing at. Then, how can we work our lives around that.

The most important thing to remember is that these are not facts. They are the stories we tell ourselves. When we tell ourselves something day in, day out, we start to believe it and then we embody and live our perceived reality. If we really wanted to, it is totally within our power to change any of these stories that we tell ourselves.

Useful mantra: I am brilliant, I am strong, I am amazing, I am happy.

LIVING IN ALIGNMENT

Once I started to understand the principles, I realised that I had to take a look at what I was doing in my work and business, and see what was in alignment with my strengths, values and character.

Positive Psychology has an amazing variety of tools that help you identify your strengths, values and character. Living in alignment means that everything we do feeds into something that enriches our life, or nourishes our soul. When we live IN alignment with who we are, life feels like a breeze. Everything we do is so in tune with who we are, we don't have to force anything, or hustle, or push ourselves. We are truly in alignment with who we are so what we do flows from us with ease and grace.

Going back to when I was studying successful people, this was absolutely something that they all had in common. They were living in alignment with who they truly were. This meant that their business or purpose, was a true calling from within, and when something feels that right, it isn't even hard work. This doesn't only apply to entrepreneurs and business people by the way. Some of the most aligned people I have ever worked with, have worked in primary schools, or animal shelters, or for charities. Because these roles are truly in alignment with who these people are as unique individuals, their work roles fulfilled them completely, and actually enhanced their existence and therefore their wellbeing.

The more I learnt, the more I realised that I had to start letting go of the limiting beliefs I had about myself, and to lean into the fact that I was brilliant at some things, and that it was ok to say I was brilliant! It felt so uncomfortable at first. *Who do I think I am to start calling myself brilliant? Get back in your box, Faye, no one wants to listen to you going on about yourself.*

My pattern of behaviour at this point was still to go to working whenever I felt I needed to escape.

Tired = work

Upset = work

Stressed = work

Trapped/lonely/scared = work

At the time, I thought this was brilliant! I told myself that my work ethic was fantastic and I was to be congratulated because I was achieving great things materially. Which is all fine - until it's not. When you're operating at this level, the wheels always fall off eventually. It is not sustainable.

It got to the third lockdown, and I was pretty close to burnout. I felt as though I was trying to keep everything going while the ground was moving underneath me. As always, on the face of it, everything seemed great. I was buying properties left right and centre. I was being offered fantastic speaking opportunities, attracting fantastic invest-ments and generally being successful.

I was also tired, upset, tearful, frustrated, empty and living completely unaligned with who I was.

This is the point where I had the walk in the woods, and I was given the idea of the *Positive Living Movement.* I knew what

I needed to do. I had to go back and apply all the things I knew to myself, and then go forth and share it with as many people as I possibly could. If I could turn things around completely, so could anyone else. Just that realisation felt so exciting, so liberating and so *right*.

There is a moment when purpose hits you in the face. And this was it.

The *Positive Living Movement* was born and everything changed. From the very start, I could not have dreamed about the amount of people who would join, and understand the whole purpose of *the Positive Living Movement*. It literally makes my heart sing. I began sharing the exercises and interventions with the online community and before I knew it, I was being offered speaking engagements (literally my favourite thing to do!), podcast guest slots, interviews, workshops, seminars and radio interviews. These are so truly my favourite things.

As soon as I was in alignment with myself, the opportunities came flooding my way.

HAPPINESS IS A SCIENCE - THE SCIENCE OF HAPPINESS

These are what works for me. The same things will not work for you - you're not me!

- Early rising

- Alcohol free
- Cold showers
- Morning routine
- Working out how to have boundaries
- Saying no!
- Say yes (to the right things)
- Pushing past my comfort zone
- Putting myself out there
- Being more
- Taking up space
- Mantras, meditation and affirmations
- Long walks

I was working with a client yesterday and she was telling me how much she enjoys playing netball with her team once a week. She never fancies going - she feels tired, it's a bit dark, she has too much housework (you know the drill!). She pushes herself to go, and absolutely love it every single time.

She said to me today, *'when I'm there, it's like nothing else exists. I am so in the game, that I'm not thinking or worrying about anything else, It's almost as if time stops.'* And that, is what being IN the moment is all about.

What is so exciting about positive psychology, is that it is a science. The techniques, interventions and exercises, are all scientifically tested and proven. We know that everyone can benefit, no matter what their circumstances or beliefs.

We are simple yet complex beings. We live absolutely in our habits. The longer we have been doing our daily routines, the stronger those neural pathways are. What is exciting though, is that it is totally possible to change them. If our current circumstances and situation is not making us happy, fulfilled and satisfied, it is absolutely, totally and simply easy and possible to start making changes.

Have you ever noticed, that so many people who have a message to share, have been through something traumatic? Breakdown, an accident, a near-death experience? This is no coincidence! When you have come back and flourished after a huge experience like that, it is the best feeling ever. In a life where you may not have been in control before, you suddenly realise that by taking back your own power, you can shape your own future and destiny. There is nothing more powerful than that! It is a golden moment and it is no wonder that so many of us are compelled to share this with as many people as possible so they can benefit too.

Many years ago, during a sound meditation, I had a visit from a robed young God. He smiled and beckoned to me. As I stepped forward, he pulled back huge curtains and there, right in front of me, was a crowd of thousands of people. It was the most incredible feeling in the world. I had a huge smile, and I felt as though I was bathed in a golden light. I felt energised, and as though at that moment, I was completely in the right place.

Our subconscious minds are so much more powerful than we will ever be. We are being sent messages all the time and we so often just let those passing thoughts drift by without acknowledging them. Listen to them. They have a powerful message for you.

Useful mantra: The point of power is always in the present moment.

WHAT'S IN IT FOR YOU?

This is where we go back to the life jacket analogy. You are the most important person in your life. That's not just ok to say, it is absolutely vital. It's not selfish, or egotistical. You need to be the best *you* can be, so you can be the best you for those around you. Once you give yourself permission to prioritise yourself, everyone around you will benefit exponentially. We have been so conditioned over time to put ourselves lower and lower down the list of priorities, and now we know how damaging this is for society as a whole. If you are being the best version of you, everyone benefits. Your children, your family, your partner, your friends.

It is a choice. That is the part that so many of us really don't realise. We look at others who seem to have it all, and think how lucky they are that their life turned out like that. Life does NOT turn out like that. It is always a choice. How much you exercise, how much you socialise, how much time you do or don't spend watching TV. The choice is yours, and how you make your choices entirely dictates what your life is going to look like.

Do what I did, look at the people you admire, and find out what they do. What are the similarities? What do their routines look like? There are inspirational people from all walks of life: all nationalities, all cultures, all abilities and disabilities, all orientations, all religions, all shapes and all sizes. There will be someone you resonate with.

Your limitations are no longer your limitations, they are your opportunities. Your blocks are no longer your blocks, they are your stepping stones. Your fears are no longer your fears, they are your motivation. I can't wait to see what the future has in store for you.

Useful mantra: It's not fear, it's excitement.

NOW IS YOUR CHANCE

If there is one thing I would like you to take away from this chapter, it is that now is always the perfect time to start. The power is always in the present moment. You are worth it. You will benefit. You do have time. And you deserve to be the most amazing version of you that you can be.

You've got this.

ABOUT THE AUTHOR

FAYE EDWARDES

Faye is the Founder of the Positive Living Movement, and a Master Positive Psychology coach who works with people all over the world to help them find their own version of happiness using positive psychology techniques and her award-winning coaching programme, FLOURISH.

Having spent many years working in sustainability, Faye discovered the power of positive psychology and how much it can transform your life and mindset. Faye is also a qualified sound therapist, a reiki practitioner, a meditation leader and a NED for a number of local and national charities.

Faye is a podcast host, author, public speaker and has been a successful property developer for the last 15 years. Faye is passionate about sustainability, is most at home in nature, spends a lot of time on the beach with her dog and is a proud mama to two wonderful children.

Faye is available for motivational speaking, podcast and radio interviews, and always welcomes exciting new opportunities.

You can reach Faye at:

Email: hello@fayeedwardes.co.uk

Facebook:

www.facebook.com/groups/positivelivingmovement

Website: www.fayeedwardes.co.uk

instagram.com/faye_positivelivingmovement

3

AN UNBREAKABLE BOND: A MOTHER, A SON, A JOURNEY

RACHAEL PARLAND

In Loving Memory of Rocco aged 5-years

'Your story may not have a happy beginning but that does not make you who you are. It is the rest of your story, who you choose to be!'

Hello beautiful souls

We all have personal histories to share, marked by anecdotes of highs and lows, be it good or bad it's our past that shapes us, we can allow 'our story' to define us or we can make significant changes to grow and become the best version of ourselves. The choice is ours.

This is my journey, that of loss, the trials and tribulations I faced losing my beloved son Rocco aged five and the choices I made to heal and determine my life and make it really worth living; one free from pain and heartache. I hope you find some inspiration from my story and appreciate that anything is possible.

My destiny was not to live a life of sorrow but that of love, hope, gratitude, abundance and positivity. A life where I am thankful for what I am, what I had, what I have and for the wisdom and experience gained along my path to which I can now share with others facing adversity. I am a mother of four children, one heavenly angel – Rocco and three earth angels Lucca, Bella-Lucia and Roma-Cia. I love each one unconditionally with all of my being. I am incredibly lucky to have them all in my heart.

I'm guessing by picking up this book, you too are looking for change? Maybe this is your journey of healing and to that of freedom? This isn't a coincidence my dear friend; you are where you are supposed to be, here with me, in your lane, on your journey, heading exactly in the correct direction. Take this as a sign if you will, a push from the Universe, your loved one, the Angels, The Divine, your Higher Self, whoever you wish your higher force to be. My intentional prayer is that my chapter offers you guidance in your healing.

I am an advocate of mindfulness and being in the present. Of course, memories are a significant part of who we are but living in the present is far more joyous, therefore my story begins where I am today.

Living in the present, I begin my mornings by creating sixty minutes for myself before my tribe get up. Grounding myself with a morning ritual which includes journaling, meditation, gratitude, self-love Reiki and exercise. This ritual derives from The 'Miracle Morning' a book that changed my life. I get up before the morning breaks and the noise begins, by setting daily intentions I prepare my mind for the day ahead, my ritual has brought my attention to so many possibilities, has cleansed my energy, helped me surrender and has given me more clarity into my future Dharma of healing others who too have faced adversity - I thank you!

'Positive vibes only' is my motto.

I've recently began to raise my vibrations by becoming an Intuitive healer and Holistic Well-being coach and mentor which will add to my previous modalities. I have become a lunar liver, where I carry out twice monthly moon rituals – I surrender what no longer serves me and set intentions for the coming moon cycle – a very old tradition that feels fit for me at present. Crystals are forming part of my life alongside yoga, meditation, Shiatsu Massage and Ayurveda - all very apt with my future goal of hosting healing retreats. Life is good!

But let's rewind back to 30th September 2006, the day my life changed forever, the day I faced every mother's worst nightmare.

Rocco had been unwell all summer, not eating, lethargic, not himself, many a night he'd wake up with a spiking temperature and was sick. I took him to the GP numerous times and was told it was *'just viral'*. Mothers' intuition, call it what you will but I was not happy and continued to hound the doctors, pushing for more tests – nothing!

September came and I will never forget his first day in Year 2, I asked him how his day had gone, only to hear his timid reply that he'd been tired and spent most of his break times sat on the wall. That breaks my heart, I made him go to school as I thought it was nothing, I was assured by the local doctors and pediatricians at the hospital he was *just fine*. He never went back to school after that first day. My mum looked after him for the rest of the month whilst I worked – I had no choice, I had a mortgage to pay and all that comes with it, plus I did not know how this would take a turn for the worst.

I got a phone call at work on 30th September, I had to go to the hospital, Rocco had, had a seizure. My poor mum had to deal with it alone. When I got to the hospital Rocco was in A & E, they allowed me in, he was being resuscitated. Just seeing his slight body, covered in tubes, with medical staff all around him made me crumble, I couldn't breathe. It was surreal. I was a complete wreck. I was ushered into a waiting room as I was getting in the way of them doing their job.

It was like being on a film, you know the one, when the actress is in the waiting room and the doctors come in and say *'I'm sorry love...'* it was unbearable, my head was falling off, I couldn't breathe, console myself, understand what was going on. I just paced the floor, over and over again. Using my mantras, telling myself, *'Everything is fine, everything is fine.'*

After what seemed like a lifetime, a pediatric consultant came into the room and we were told that Rocco was stable, but not out of the woods. I felt the biggest sigh of relief and thanked my lucky stars. We were 'Blue-lighted' to Alder Hey where the diagnosis began to unfold. Rocco was diagnosed with Leukemia - It later transpired that Rocco actually had a rare *adult* blood disease (ITP) never *ever* seen in a child before, hence it going unnoticed - the leukemia was a trigger from that.

If only we had got to the ITP first as the Chemotherapy treatment did nothing to help with the primary condition, it only hindered the situation – nobody knew what to do, having no previous cases as such anywhere in the whole wide world, the consultants had no protocol to follow, looking back now I would have done things differently, such as halting the chemotherapy and treating the dominant condition – hindsight is a beautiful theory.

I had begun my *Law of Attraction* journey long before Rocco's illness, 'The Secret' was my starting point and I enjoyed practiced the LOA, albeit not to the extent I do now. Whilst Rocco was in hospital, I kept saying to him, *'Everything will be fine, we are together forever'*. When anybody telephoned me I responded in a similar way *'Yes, all's good, he's doing brilliant'*. Being positive was crucial, I could not allow negative thoughts to enter my mind, *'Ask, Believe, Receive'*, 'The Secret' told me and that, I trusted. I also begged God to answer my prayers.

Being in hospital was a roller coaster of a journey, both ups and downs, to be told one minute Rocco wouldn't make it, to see him sat up in bed the following day asking for a fried breakfast.

Watching him begging for water but not being able to give him any due to having to monitor his fluid intake was torture. He was given an ice cube in a capped tumbler at one point. Sometimes I'd think 'F$*k it' and seeing his grateful, cheeky face smiling, knowing we had been bad, made it all worthwhile.

I had to learn new ways to cook, potassium free and the daily long haul dialysis trips which drained me completely, were beginning to take the toll on Rocco's poor little body.

Remembering the moments of bringing him strength makes me beam, he had to take copious amounts of medication but with my motivation it was usually a success. We had so many conversations over our stay at Alder Hey, one being me promising him a dog when we returned home – he even chose the type (I've still got the photograph of it), it was a Husky – not my choice – but I vowed.

We were advised we could come home for Halloween; we were overjoyed, I knew this is what he needed as he had been prodded and poked for so long and possibly confused about the whole situation being so small. I had his bedroom newly furnished, and I was super excited to show him his new 'Captain's bunk'.

Sadly, that time never came, he got severe diarrhoea, Jacqueline, my sister decorated his room *'Halloween style'*, it was the best in the hospital he was thrilled to bits, his smile said it all, he was proud as punch.

When he was moved to ICU they wouldn't let me stay overnight, I remember being woken in the middle of the night, I thought that was *'the call'* I sprinted over, they said he wouldn't settle – he was incubated, awake yet unable to communicate which must have been dreadful and frightening– Rocco looked up at me, *'Everything OK?'* I asked. He shook his head, *'What's up pal?'* I knew by now, as he'd been incubated for some time what he would want, it was a process of elimination. He couldn't move himself due to muscle wastage so usually he needed turning or had a bad itch. That night he had an itchy leg.

I knew everything about him, I cared for him 24/7, I did it all. He was my boy and I couldn't (or maybe wouldn't) allow the nurses to care for him as I looked on, I was on 24 hour call, I was exhausted, I changed his bedding myself, bathed him, fed him and when his muscles wasted away I turned him as and when he asked and throughout the night as his days and nights became one. He was tortured throughout the process and it was excruciatingly painful and agonising for me as I watched on helpless.

Seeing him incubated whilst still awake was horrendous, I still wonder why they didn't sedate him, instead he was given Midazolam, (AKA - The date rape drug) to make this easier for him. However, this caused more distress as every time he came round he thought he was choking, I had to repeat the same story, if not more than 1000 times over the duration. *'It's OK, we just have a tube down your throat to help you breath, you are OK my baby'* .

The vision still haunts me now and will continue to do so until the day I die. What must have been going through that small head of his?

Towards Rocco's final days I was advised that *yet again* he had septicaemia – he'd beaten it twice previously before but nevertheless each time was as painful as the next, both were touch and go situations, at times they were uncertain he'd make it but the little fighter always bounced back.

This time his line had caused the infection and he needed an operation to replace it. I was advised his body was too weak to make it through the operation this time round but neither of us were giving up. *'You can do this'* I said *'Can't you?'*, his little head nodded, he kept his promise God bless him and I was overjoyed to see him return from the operating theatre, albeit he was not conscious, he had held on for me and I will *never ever* forget our last conversation and the fact that he kept his promise. God love him.

I was advised he would not make it through the night, it was just a matter of time. His tiny body was covered in numerous tubes, his tummy swollen like a balloon due to retaining water, we didn't know if he was in pain or not. I begged the nurses on that final day, jumping out of the bed asking, *'Can you try this? 'Can you try that?' 'What about this?' 'What about that?'*, I had lost everything in my power, I just couldn't accept that there was nothing more they could do for my darling boy. I must have jumped up about 25-30 times, if not more that final night with suggestions.

The poor nurse on duty couldn't cope any longer with my pain and had to swap with her colleague, I was desperate, clutching at straws, hoping, praying, begging that one of my suggestions just might be the answer to saving him. The last breath he took, or when his spirit soul left his body was my last hope, only to be told, he had gone. I held him in my arms for the next six hours, until I was removed from the room, I slept with him in my arms the whole time.

My prayers were not answered that night, my life was in pieces, my heart broken into two.

The day Rocco grew his wings is a day that will haunt me forever and my life changed instantly. I cannot change what happened and I've learned throughout my healing journey that somethings, I must accept, no matter how hard.

In this situation, there's only one way, you sink my beautiful soul or you swim and I for one did just that, I swam and swam and swam and swam. Obviously at the beginning I was drowning, it was horrifically painful and terribly hard, but I kept on swimming.

I feel the journey Rocco and I went through in itself is one I would love to share in my own book on a greater scale but that story is one of love, hope, pain, torture, sorrow, togetherness, ups, downs, living away from home, one horrendous diagnosis, four different consultants with no idea what to do, learning as they went, trying everything in their power only to sadly fail, not through love nor trying. This chapter, however, is about my journey following the tragedy, the journey of courage, hope, love, survival and that of light.

I hope that my story will bring you honesty, strength, hope, love, and self-belief, that anything is possible, even on the darkest of days, there is always a light at the end of the tunnel. My intention is to guide you through the coping mechanisms I used along the winding path I took whilst healing. If it's your saving grace, I weep with joy, maybe a signpost if you like in helping you through a difficult, painful or challenging time, whatever you take from this, I hope you find some inspiration. If you have been through any adversity, you will know how I feel - reach out. If there were tools as such for me whilst I was going through the most turbulent time I ever faced, I would have been eternally grateful.

Rocco's departure was heart wrenching, I was broken, I just wanted to curl up and die. I had a numbness which impaired my ability to function. For nano seconds each morning I awoke, I was fine, I was me, then it hit me like a ton of bricks, I'd lost my son, it was like ground hog day. I just didn't want to get up, I wanted the day over before it began.

Then I found myself questioning my loss and feeling angry towards others. I'd look at a lady who lived down the road from me who had twins (forgive me if you are reading this) and thought *why not her, she's got two children who are the same?* Everywhere I turned I was reminded of my loss, everything on TV related to me, someone had lost a child, someone was grieving, there were lots of children a similar age – I couldn't be free of it and to top it off everyone was carrying on with their lives as per normal enjoying life and I'd just had my life ripped apart - Rocco had his life cut short, he'd been robbed as had I.

I was infuriatingly angry; I blamed the hospital for not doing their job properly, myself - had I missed something? Should I have said 'NO' to the chemotherapy whilst we sorted the primary condition out?

Predominantly, I felt that I had died and that someone had forgotten to bury me. I wished the years away, as I knew that as time went by, things wouldn't get easier but the pain would be more bearable because I'd get accustomed to a *'new way of living'* without him.

'Time is a healer.'

When people used to say this to me, I felt like ripping their head off, my blood would boil– how dare they? Who were they to tell me that in time I will be OK losing my son?

But believe me, with time comes healing, with time comes self-development and with time comes learning how to cope with a massive hole in your heart.

You don't *ever* get over it, but by implementing intentions and coping mechanisms and taking action into making these strategies work for you, life becomes more bearable, trust me.

It's very apt to mention my marvelous mum here, *'my rock'* as she too felt the pain I was feeling, having helped raise Rocco from an early age whilst I worked. My mum is the most self-less lady I know, she was with me at the hospital from the outset, from the moment Rocco was whisked away in the ambulance to Alder Hey. I followed in my car, thinking we would all be coming back together, sadly this wasn't to be. My mum gave up everything for me during Rocco's diagnosis and following his death nothing changed, she supported me daily.

It was around March time when my mum suggested joining the gym, I'd never been an advocate for any form of exercise before but it sounded like a plan and what an excellent form of therapy it was. I worked out most days and began eating healthy, focusing on some self-love and eventually qualifying as a fitness instructor. My sister Jacqueline would come weekly, we would cry and reminisce, and this too was good for my soul, being able to talk about him freely, let it all out— she was such a good listener. I had some good friends, its times as such when you realise who your true friends are. Leanne my oldest friend of all time mothered me most weekends, I just hated being alone.

After family support, during those early bleak months came counseling which helped tremendously. I sought several different agencies until I found the right lady for me. Cruise Counseling, North Wales started me on my healing journey. By speaking out and seeking help from others, I realised that it didn't make me weak, it made me human. I would not be here today if I hadn't reached out for help. It was by stepping into the unknown, taking whatever resources I could get my hands that helped me on my journey to true healing.

I would like to share a simile that my counsellor shared with me, something that I will never forget and looking back she was right, it was *'The Ball and the Box analogy'*.

"Grief is like a bouncing ball, even if you handle it with care, it will still hit the walls of your life and that pain button that sounds the alarm. It may feel like your pain is never going to end and that the huge ball leaves no room for anything else in your life. However, that ball that currently feels so large and present has a tiny escape valve. It'll eventually start losing air".

The counsellor I am discussing was my second, seeking the right person to share how I felt worked wonders for me, just off loading what I encountered that week, what I faced, what I was up against, where my emotions were at. The councilor had not lost her child, therefore at times I thought, *What does she know?* She had however, lost her husband. I got to know her well over time, she had been through grief and albeit not her son, a dear loved one at that, she also felt pain – the most she had ever felt, this wasn't a competition who'd lost the most, this was her most and so a part of me began to heal. I didn't know then, but the nourishing of my soul was commencing.

During my lowest ebb I read countless books about mothers who had similar stories, such as *'And still I Rise'* (Lawrence, 2006), *'I let him go'* (Bulger, 2018), *'Goodbye, Dearest Holly'*, (Wells, 2005) not to mention but a few. These mothers too had gone through horrendous traumas, some couldn't drag themselves out of the ditch, others grew strength and hope, some held bitterness, guilt and extreme pain and just couldn't move on. I knew that holding onto bitterness, blaming others and feeling guilty would only create a poison which would eat me alive.

I'm a firm believer that bitterness it like a Cancer to your body and that I had to let go of any resentment and surrender to move forward. During this time, I also began reading around the subject of Buddhism. I'm no Buddhist by any means but I have read around the topic for many years now and implement it into my daily being, I just love the ideology behind it, it's incredible. If we took a leaf or two from the concept of Buddhism, we could all live harmonious lives.

I got completely lost in books, they helped me forget about the current, brutal situation I was facing and gave my head the much-needed rest from the noise both external and internal. I could have been anyone whilst reading, occasionally my mind would remind me how cruel the world was but then I got back into a book and was once again lost.

'Your thoughts become things' (The Secret, 2006)

Over time I began to wake and tell myself in the mirror a form of *Affirmation*, that *'Today was going to be a good day'* – did I believe it? No! But it made me feel better and so I continued with this mantra daily. It began to form part of my morning ritual. I began to contact local groups to meet with other bereft parents, I sought clairvoyants, went to spiritual churches and visited Rocco's garden daily, and I mean every single day without fail - it became an obsession which I've learnt to relax with over time, taking peace knowing he is with me always, my very own guardian angel!

I knew going back to work was not an option, I didn't want to face anybody. I worked in the corporate world as Operations Manager. When redundancy was offered, I jumped at the chance - the universe had my back – the universe knew where my journey was heading and right then I needed to heal. Always trust the process, you are where you are meant to be at any given time.

I accepted redundancy and enrolled onto a University Degree (who would have thought!) It gave me no time to sit and dwell as all day, every day and I was studying hard, head down, best grades coming in. I was on my biggest self-development journey and continuing on my road to healing.

Going to University meant meeting lots of new people and with that the dreaded question, *'Do you have children?'* This caused me incredible pain to begin with. I remember going to my mum and balling my eyes out that I had told somebody that I had no children. I felt I'd let Rocco down. Of course, I had a child but I didn't want to deal with the questions that followed. My mum and I mulled it over and we decided that in future I'd say, *'Yes I have one child'* and then change the subject quickly, of which I did several times before people would want to prolong the conversation about my child. I didn't want to tell people straight away on meeting them, that I had lost a child and start crying – they'd think I was absolutely bonkers. Following another discussion/team chat, my mum and I decided that I would say *'Yes, I have an angel child who I lost when he was five, however, I would rather not discuss this further'*. It worked, Rocco was not hidden away and no one felt the need to probe any further. Obviously when friendships were made I was able to discuss Rocco but it was my decision when that time was right. I wasn't put on the proverbial spot.

When studying at university, my inner voice would pipe up intermittently, questioning who I thought I was and exclaiming that *'I wasn't clever enough to be a university student'*. Limiting beliefs are prevalent for everyone but knowing how to dismiss them is even more triumphant, this is another coping mechanism that I have gained on my journey and one that I love to share with others, I know my worth and what I am capable of and everyone can claim their right to *'boycott the inner bitch'*.

University brought many ups and downs from tears of despair and the limiting beliefs that *'I wasn't clever enough'*, to walking out with a First-class BA (Honours) in Social Policy and Politics. I wanted nothing less – I was doing this for my boy. I then went on and did a Postgraduate in Education. I put my heart and soul into my studies, and this helped me massively through the worse time of my life. I am not suggesting that anybody going through adversity should quit their job and go to University but finding a hobby, enrolling on a course, or getting engrossed in something that you are truly passionate about could be helpful. That feeling of growth and my mind being busy contributed to the factors of my healing process.

I would never have believed that I would be where I am today, I am truly grateful for the progress I have made and anybody who has faced adversity can do this also with help. I was prescribed incredibly difficult dealings, but it is through these struggles that I have risen and through my endeavors to heal and grow that I have become who I am meant to be and you my beautiful friend, no matter what life throws at you can rise too.

'Do I want Rocco here right now?', Of course – I would give my right arm, leg, all limbs.

'Will that happen? No.

'Would he want me to be sad for the rest of my life?' I know he wouldn't.

'Would being sad help my children, would it help anyone?' No.

I think the answers to these are me playing devil's advocate. I had to dig deep, incredibly deep, deeper than deep but I dug and I dug and I dug and I dug.

The coping/healing strategies I used and practice still today, such as visualization, setting tangible intentions, self-love, living fearlessly, clearing out limiting beliefs are all tools which turned my life around into one worth living, one I love and one I am truly grateful for. This is just an insight, a point in the right direction if you like to hopefully give others that may be facing adversity some hope.

I have no magic wand, you can't *'skip the steps'* that grief, trauma or any adversity creates. There are no short cuts and I cannot take any credit for the teachings I share either - this wisdom has been passed onto me for which I am truly grateful for and I will continue to share the wealth of knowledge I have acquired within my future career in Intuitive Healing and Coaching.

Child loss is not an event but an indescribable journey of survival. Our emotions are in place to keep us safe and so once we are in tune with them, the better we can deal with given situations, the easier those bearings will become. You cannot remain positive at all times, that is a misconception, sometimes things are unbearable, but it is how we go about trudging through them that matters.

My sister sent me this quote and I will never forget the peace it brought me.

'You are energy, and energy cannot be created or destroyed. Energy just changes form. The true essence of You, the pure energy of You, has always been and will always be. You can never not be'. (The Secret, 2006). Thank you Gail.

I will see my boy again, that I know for sure as everything is energy – Rocco's energy is out there somewhere!

The loss of my child has not defined me, but it has certainly changed me forever. There are some souls who bring light so great to the world that even after they have gone, the light remains. I still grieve but am grateful of where I am today, that I had the strength and courage to take hold of my life and turn it around. Do I feel guilty? No! It doesn't mean Rocco is any less loved, it means I am giving myself a chance at the life I should have had.

No mother should bury her child before herself, it's not the right order. I get that, but additionally I can't give up, I have a legacy to create and I would love to help others through trauma, loss, self-belief, fear, mindset and adversity with my growing coaching abilities.

No matter what type of adversity we go through, we deserve to live a life of abundance, choose courage, be fearless and say yes to opportunities. We all have the power to set ourselves free. The work towards freedom is by no means easy but it is most definitely worthwhile.

We are in control of our own destiny – we must set intentions and rid ourselves of limiting beliefs that *'we cannot do this'*, because we *can*. I believe that whatever path we are on it is our own journey, no two paths are the same, we must trust the process and not rush it. We will all get there when the time is right!

I love Rocco, God bless his soul, but he is resting easy now with his grandfathers, that I have had to accept, release and along the way heal – everyday isn't one of ease but the days I do feel free I am truly grateful for.

I have found this process both difficult and liberating, I have wept, both tears of heartbreak and that of joy, seeing how far I have come as this healing process has allowed me to reflect on the milestones I have conquered along the way. I am thankful and appreciative that you have heard my journey and I hope some of my vulnerability, experiences and coping mechanisms resonate. I would like to thank you from the depth of my soul for allowing me the honour of your precious time, I feel truly humbled and grateful . My connection to the universe has helped me massively, I have learned that our lowest of lows can eventually bring about blessings and that the storms will create sunshine eventually. It has made me who I am today. We can't control everything that happens to us, but we can control how we respond.

I will never forget the love I have for my child, Rocco as he lives on in myself, his siblings and my everlasting memories. Overtime time and by healing I have become more liberated, and I find as time goes on, these days become more so.

Maybe I was meant to lose Rocco and that's bittersweet, perhaps he was too good for earth and that I was supposed to go through this turmoil, distress, heartache, pain – call it what you will, to make me who I am today and to help others on their healing journeys. Maybe I am your lightworker. They say God only distributes what one can handle, if so, I wish I wasn't strong enough to rise from such pain and then I would still have my boy today. When I look how far I have come, I now know I am capable of anything.

From the ashes I rose and for that I thank the Universe and my Angel Rocco who, this chapter would not have been possible without.

I write this in Rocco's memory, in his honour on the year of his 21st birthday– Son, this is for you – I love you immensely - until we meet again!

ABOUT THE AUTHOR

RACHAEL PARLAND

Rachael Parland is an Intuitive healer and Holistic Well-being coach and mentor within the health and wellness industry.

As a master of mindset, manifesting, limiting beliefs, spirituality, lunar living and business strategies, Rachael combines, numerous years of coaching and self-developing to support, coach and mentor people that have not only suffered loss but those wanting transformational change.

By changing one's mindset and setting clear intentions, Rachael advocates that we all deserve to live a life which includes self-love, abundance, joy and purpose and whatever stage you are on your journey to live a better life, by removing old habits and limiting beliefs and becoming the best version of yourself both personally and professionally.

Having qualified in the fitness industry during her early years she moved into the Corporate World, Managing, Coaching Mentoring and Developing staff within her realm. After tragically losing her five-year-old beloved child Rocco, Rachael realised she needed to find a more fulfilling purpose in life. Beginning a six year-long study, Rachael became a lecturer in Social Policy and Travel and Tourism.

As she healed, she began her journey of healing by introducing Mindfulness, Yoga, Meditation, Mindset and the Law of Attraction. Following her Dharma, she met a Spiritual Healer who began to peel back her layers, she was introduced to the world of Spirituality, Reiki (currently seeking her Masters Qualification), Lunar living, Crystal Energy, Massage and Ayurveda.

She is a NLP and Belief Code registered facilitator and offers a whole host of soul centred heart led treatments of both traditional and modern styles.

Rachael is incredibly passionate about sharing her journey, experience and knowledge to inspire others into finding gratification and self-worth for life despite the adversity they may have faced.

You can find out more about working with Rachael at:

Email: magikwand07@aol.com

Facebook: Rachael Rocco

facebook.com/Rachael_Rocco

instagram.com/rachaelparland

4

FREE TO BE ME

ROXY KING-CLARK

*N*owadays I feel free to be me.

I no longer dream of being confident; I finally have the confidence I've longed for my whole life.

I'm able to be unapologetically me; I know who I am and I embrace it.

I fully understand myself and my inner self talk is so kind and I no longer berate myself.

For the first time in my life I have a career that truly fulfils me and lights me up. My business is growing and I'm thoroughly enjoying the journey. Work-life balance is a top priority for me. I work from home and so I'm able to be there for my two young sons as I work when they're at school, with grandparents and in bed.

FREE TO BE ME

Until now I'd floated through life not really knowing what I wanted to do. Now I feel fired up and passionate about what I do. I have a business where I help fellow female business owners with their social media marketing and menstrual health. An unlikely combination you may think. But our menstrual cycle is, of course, an integral part of being a woman and despite what society would have us think is not a negative part of being a woman. With the right help and support we can embrace our cycle and work with it - not against it.

I'm now no longer overpowered and controlled by my anxiety. My life is not dictated to by anxiety. My anxiety doesn't keep me at home too scared to go out. My anxiety hasn't – yet – completely disappeared but I do now know what caused it, what triggers it and now that I understand it, I'm able to give myself grace, compassion and support.

I'm also able to freely speak up about how anxiety has affected, and still affects, my life.

But it hasn't always been like this.

CHALLENGES

Anxiety has been a challenge I've faced for over twenty years. At times it has completely dictated my life. It was usually at the centre of the dark times in my life. I used to frequently experience low days for what seemed to be for no apparent reason. At times my anxiety left me feeling paralysed by fear and unable to leave my house. My feet felt glued to the spot as the anxiety took over.

Even before my anxiety started, I've never been particularly kind to myself. I've always been my own worst critic. My inner self talk was brutal and I was so unnecessarily hard on myself. I previously always prided myself on being a perfectionist, I even had it on my CV! Now I joke that I'm a recovering perfectionist. 'Done is better than perfect' is my motto and I embrace imperfect action. Moving away from that impossible gold standard has been freeing in more ways than I could ever imagine.

If I could speak to my younger self, I would tell her to be kind to herself. I would tell her to get help for the anxiety much sooner. There was no need to suffer like that for all those years. I would also tell her to speak out, anxiety is nothing to be ashamed of. And that my feelings are valid and important.

I never spoke up about how my anxiety affected me. I put on a mask and tried to cover it up. I'd come up with an excuse for why I couldn't do something. That helped me to stay safe but it didn't help me to deal with my anxiety. If we hide how we're feeling and don't open-up then we can't move forward; as individuals and as society.

I was born in the Falkland Islands, only four years after the 1982 Conflict, I have no doubt that this has influenced various aspects of my life. I have always been very aware of the sacrifices made for our freedom and the true horror that people experienced (and how many are still affected to this day). They had something real to deal with. What I *'went through'* was nothing in comparison, I just needed to *get over it* or *get on with it.* Which was not a view I would've held for anyone else other than myself. Everyone has their own challenges and struggles to face. Their thoughts and feelings are valid. Just as mine were and are.

Each time I see someone speak out about anxiety or any other mental health challenge I feel inspired. I hope that by writing about my experiences that I can help and inspire others. When you're in the thick of it you can feel hopeless, like there's no way out and that you're the only one feeling like this. I assure you though, there is hope, there is a way out and you're not alone.

I applaud anyone who speaks up about any mental health challenge, but I also understand those who are not yet ready. Do it in your own time. Find people or a place to share where you feel safe. I never had any desire to speak up about my anxiety. I hoped that it would fade out and not be an issue again. That was very wishful thinking. What I needed was to find support, take action and help myself.

It was only by luck that it did happen. I did find support and get help and I did the work. I was finally able to heal. I am now able to talk about the whole of my experience from the scar, not the wound. And I'm ready to tell my story.

Dreams

As a kid I had so many big dreams. As I got older I no longer held the same dreams. Which would've been fine, but they weren't replaced with new ones. I had lots of things that I enjoyed but I had no real passion for anything. Which I didn't even notice at the time, I just happily went along with life. I enjoyed different jobs and had some amazing opportunities, but that passion and drive was missing.

For so long I lacked self-confidence and self-belief. And so even if the passion had been there the lack of confidence and belief to make it a reality was missing. My limiting beliefs held me back and kept me nice and safe; firmly in my comfort zone. I turned down opportunities, settled for less and made stupid decisions.

I strove for unrealistic perfection and I overthought everything. If I made a mistake then I would obsess about it, feel embarrassed and berate myself. I'm still working on letting go of what others think of me. But I'm not as hyper-sensitive as to what people think about me. I put up with being treated badly by others for fear of not being liked.

When my eldest son started school, I was highly anxious about it for many months leading up to it. The anxiety got worse and worse the nearer the time came. I thought it was just because I was going to miss him and it was a big next step for us all. But I realised that it was because I'd been triggered by him going into the same education system that had let me down. Yes, the rational part of me knew that a lot had changed in the past twenty years but my trauma response resurfaced and I felt so scared. I feared him not being treated well, or him being sad and scared and feeling abandoned by me.

I was panicking thinking not just about him starting school but the many years of education ahead of him. What if he was bullied or what if he got ill? What if he felt trapped at school and couldn't get out? There being only one primary school and one secondary school in our community would we have to take him out of school and home school him or would we have to move so he could attend a different school? My mind went into complete overdrive and I spiralled. Thankfully my husband was there to support me and we worked through it together. By the time it came for our son to start school I was in a much better place and he settled in after a few weeks. The following year when our youngest son started school I didn't have the anxiety as I'd already dealt with the root cause.

I do still have to be really careful not to go back down that rabbit hole of worrying about challenges our boys may face at school. I remind myself that as a family we will get through them. I'm also thankful for my experiences as I know that I'm strong and would stand up for our boys when needed.

CHANGES

I remember how I grew up absolutely loving school. I was the 'geek' that would do extra maths tests at home for fun. I took part in public speaking competitions, was in a band, handed in my homework on time, was on the school council, was selected for special projects, was never late and I tried my best at sport – even though I wasn't much good. I always tried my hardest in every subject and in everything I did.

Until I was 14 years old.

When everything changed.

Then I became terrified of school

I had not long begun my GCSEs when I got a virus. I barely remember anything from that time, I vaguely remember being sick for a bit, but my memories are overshadowed by what followed. What I vividly remember is the two brutal years of suffering from Post Viral Fatigue Syndrome. That was when my twenty+ years of living with anxiety began.

If you've ever experienced fatigue you'll know just how debilitating it is. For those two years I was utterly exhausted, completely wiped out and pretty darn miserable. My Mum, Dad, Grandparents and Aunt pulled me through it. My Mum was my absolute rock and I'm so lucky that she's so strong and got me through the other side. She was often asked how on earth we were coping with everything, of course, there wasn't an alternative. We had to get through it and we just took it one day at a time.

Walking the three minutes to the corner shop would have me in bed for the rest of the day. Everything I did drained me. Not helped by the fact that I felt sick the whole time and struggled to eat. I was already skinny, despite a very healthy appetite, but I lost weight and by the end of the two years I could clearly see my ribs. When my appetite finally returned my Mum would feed me an English breakfast each morning as I felt ravenous – and wanted to cover up my ribs! It felt incredible to have my hunger and energy back.

My incredible Mum had to care for me whilst battling the injustice and pressure we were under. The support we received from the Education Department was extremely limited. Their lack of empathy and understanding was astounding. Some individual teachers were wonderful, particularly my kind and caring Headteacher who even gave up his office for me to do my art exams in. But because those higher up were unwilling to be supportive or to understand what I was going through then this trickled down into the school to my teachers and friends.

They always knew how much I loved school and so their reaction to me struggling absolutely baffled me. It was like they thought I'd had a personality transplant and had suddenly turned lazy and couldn't be bothered to go to school! Or that I was being a silly teenager. Or perhaps they thought I liked the attention and drama. As a shy introvert this couldn't have been further from the truth.

Whatever their thinking, the lack of empathy and support was heart-breaking, and life changing. What a difference it could have made to my experience at the time and the years since if they'd just tried to understand and be kind. I believe that if they'd provided support when I was physically ill then that would not have led into mental health issues too.

Instead, the pressure from the Education Department for me to be at school was immense. They said that I *legally* had to be in school. But it was physically, and emotionally, impossible for me to be there. As a compromise, because they insisted I had to be on school grounds for at least some of the time, they '*let me*' study in the library. But I was exhausted and highly anxious. I had to have my Mum with me the whole time for support.

I panicked at the thought of being there alone. Even now when I look back I can feel the fear.

I remember my friends and classmates coming into the library, I just wanted the ground to swallow me up. I didn't want to be different. I wanted life to go back to normal and I wanted to feel well again. I missed my old life of hanging out with friends, being active, having fun and being in school.

Thankfully the lovely librarian was amazing and so supportive; I did the majority of my exams in her storeroom cupboard of as I simply couldn't cope with being in a full classroom.

I was also forced to go in for tutor time in the hope I'd then stay for lessons. But on top of feeling completely exhausted and sick I felt trapped and panicky. I'd sneak out of the school after tutor time and walk home in tears trying not to panic. I'd be fighting against my flight survival instinct as all

I wanted to do was sprint home to safety, but I knew if I did that then the exhaustion would be even worse. Even walking home meant I'd be exhausted for the rest of the day. Sometimes my Mum would meet me in the car outside and the relief I felt was overwhelming. It felt like I'd escaped jail!

One of the worst moments during this time was receiving an email from a group of my close friends telling me that they didn't want to be my friends anymore. I can't remember the exact wording, but they basically didn't believe me, didn't understand and didn't want to be associated with me anymore. My Dad consoled me as I stood there sobbing my heart out that I'd been further cast aside and kicked down. It was another blow and it certainly didn't help me to get back into school!

The constant judgment, whispers and pressure from my classmates was awful and that feeling has stayed with me as I still (annoyingly!) worry and wonder about what others think of me.

At some point I was offered tranquilisers by the Psychiatrist (although he didn't recommend it, it was just an option put forward). I didn't even contemplate it for a moment. I knew that what I actually needed was support, understanding and no more pressure. Medication would have covered over some of the symptoms, but it wouldn't have solved the actual problems.

Between my Mum and I, and limited support from some teachers, we had to prepare me for my GCSEs. I had to drop some so I could concentrate on the core subjects. Somehow through it all I managed to pass them. Although it still really hurt to not get the high grades I'd been predicted and had consistently received throughout my school life. It was a real bittersweet moment. One that I had to relive every time I was asked for my results or went for a job interview. I had to explain what had happened and always worried people thought I was making up excuses.

LUCKY

During a bad bout of anxiety I would vow to myself that I was going to seek out help. But I never did. I would come out the other side feeling okay and with hope that this good feeling would continue. Perhaps this would be it and my anxiety would miraculously disappear. Of course, it never did and this became a constant cycle.

Instead, my pivotal moment came about by chance. I wasn't even looking for help. I took part in a free online challenge about time-blocking. The top prize was a 90-minute session with Lin Alchin, an *Empowered Self-Belief Mentor*, who I'd not long come across. I completed the challenge and was lucky enough to win the session!

But then reality hit that I was going to have to talk to and open-up to a complete stranger in New Zealand via Zoom. I was absolutely bricking it before the call. I was physically shaking with nerves and totally overthinking. *What if I made a fool of myself? What if she thought I was stupid? What if I panicked and wanted to run away?* So many thoughts, so many worries.

But I needn't have worried. She put me at ease straight away and we got on like a house on fire – and we still do. I opened up to her about my anxiety and we worked together to find out where it stemmed from. We made so many break-throughs in that session and I had so many moments of real-isation. The progress we made in that first session and the changes that came about afterwards were monumental.

There hasn't been a single time since that first session that I've been paralysed by anxiety and unable to leave my home. It was like a switch flicked in my head and the grey clouds lifted. All this worry and weight that I'd carried around for all these years lifted.

Lin had me write a letter to my group of friends who'd sent me the cruel email. I told them how the email had made me feel and the impact it had had on me. I didn't send the letter but it was a very cathartic exercise.

In all the years I had never sat down and thought about what triggered my anxiety. I'd always tried to look back on the experience from a positive angle. I'm an optimist and always look for the positives in situations. Yes, it was awful at the time but I came out the other side with more empathy for others, I learnt invaluable life skills and I was stronger and able to stand up for myself and others.

But what I'd never done before was to address the trauma (and realise that that's what it was) and its long-term ramifications. Once I actually did it seemed so blindingly obvious that my experience during those two awful years had had a major impact on my life.

Once I started the work of uncovering what was behind my anxiety and feeling it lift I knew I needed to continue this work. I began to have weekly 60 minute 1:1 sessions with Lin and continued the work of helping myself. The weight lifted more and more each day.

We started this work and this journey in June 2020 and by the August I felt inspired and confident enough to start my own business in social media marketing. I had the social media marketing experience and a Business with Marketing Management degree behind me but I threw myself in to learning as much as I could including gaining a Professional Diploma in Digital Marketing.

In January 2021 I launched my business, *Rox Your Marketing*, and opened my free Facebook community. Lin saw the potential and believed in me so much that she was my first social media management client.

Being an entrepreneur (or business owner if you're more comfortable with that term) is a huge journey of ongoing personal and professional development. I'm currently still a one woman show and have learnt to do everything myself. Since my experience of working with Lin and seeing the difference getting support can make I've continued to invest time, money and energy into myself and my business.

I never truly realised and appreciated the importance of having a strong mindset when running your own business. Now it's something I work on constantly.

Lin speaks about peeling off the layers of an onion to find what's underneath and causing you to feel the way you do. I found journaling to be a very powerful tool at helping me to peel off my layers. The combination of giving myself time to reflect and physically writing gave me endless moments of realisation which allowed me to work through things and move forwards. I would highly recommend trying it.

You can use journal prompts or you can reflect on your day/week. My favourite is to journal about issues and feelings as they arise. For example, I'd pick up my journal if I felt uneasy going to a shop, if I felt triggered by what someone had said or done or why I wanted to tackle a certain part of parenting in a particular way. Journaling allowed me to acknowledge my feelings, examine the reasons for them, work out how to react in a different way in the future if necessary, move on and not admonish myself.

When my anxiety was particularly bad, I would struggle to leave my home. I felt paralysed by fear. Which if you've never had to deal with severe anxiety like this before then it can be hard to comprehend and understand.

What was I afraid of? It's not like a lion was going to eat me on the way to the post office. I knew it wasn't logical. I struggled to articulate to my husband why I was struggling. My brain would become so overwhelmed that I couldn't think straight. All I wanted was to go to bed until it stopped.

Once these episodes were over then I just wanted to forget about them and move on. I didn't want to reflect back. I felt like such a failure and so stupid for being like that. I felt ashamed and embarrassed. I didn't even fully share with my husband how bad it was.

Once I started working with Lin and reflecting back on these times then I understood the power of reflection. Now that I'm in a much clearer space I actually rather enjoy reflecting. The moments of realisation come thick and fast and when they do I heal a bit more each time.

I hid my anxiety very well for nearly twenty years. Now I freely and openly share about my experiences. I've gone live in my Facebook group when my anxiety has flared up and I've been real, honest and vulnerable. I want people to know that they're not alone, that it's okay to talk about it and that there are ways to get better. The comments I've received from my audience have been amazing and I've been able to have some powerful conversations with people.

My anxiety wasn't a constant. At one point I was working as an Aviation Coordinator for an oil rig. It was an intense and high pressure job, that I was really good at, in a male dominated environment and I was thrown in the deep end having had no previous experience for a job like this. I was in charge of organising the crew changes for the rig with plans constantly having to change. My anxiety was never a problem.

When I reflect back now I can see that certain situations triggered my anxiety; going to a classroom, not feeling liked, feeling trapped, feeling judged, stepping out of my comfort zone, during my inner autumn (the time before my period arrives). When it was triggered I could end up sat on the floor sobbing and feeling lost and scared.

Tracking my menstrual cycle was another pivotal step. I became really tuned in to myself, both emotionally and physically. I can now identify patterns in my cycle and I use this knowledge to my advantage. For example, I know that if I don't look after myself and I overdo it then my anxiety will flare up during my inner autumn (luteal phase, right before menstruation) and I'll be in pain or uncomfortable in my inner winter (menstrual phase/period).

I'm able to take a step back and assess what I'm feeling and why. And that's hugely powerful.

As a Menstrual Cycle Coach, I help other women to do the same. I've finally found something that I'm truly passionate about. This is what I've been waiting for my whole life. I believe that our menstrual cycles are our superpower. Which I know can feel like an insane concept when so many women suffer. But this is because of society's narrative and view of it. We've been taught that it's a negative aspect of being a woman and that we just need to get on with it and suffer in silence.

But it isn't a given that it has to be like that.

There are so many ways that we can help ourselves. So many things that we should be taught. The whole of society loses when women are suppressed and unable to even talk about something so natural. Having real knowledge about our menstrual cycles is empowering. This knowledge helps girls and women, society and business.

As well as helping me personally it's also helped to further strengthen our marriage and my relationship with my boys. I feel very confident explaining why I feel a certain way and why I've reacted in a particular way. And I'll apologise if I didn't react well and then work through how to react better next time. This then helps to not be mean to myself. No one is perfect but I know that each day I'm working on myself and I'm moving forwards. It's been very powerful.

ONWARDS

Writing this chapter has been incredibly cathartic. I've uncovered more about my past than I ever imagined and I've had endless lightbulb moments as I realised where feelings and beliefs have stemmed from. I can reflect on how my life has shaped me into the person I am today. Of course, writing your story in a published book isn't an everyday thing, but thanks to this process I'm going to return to regular journaling. I would recommend journaling to anyone, you'll be amazed at what comes to the surface. Sometimes it can be painful, but if you can work through it you can start to heal. I've found for me that that's healthier than ignoring or burying the issues and feelings.

I'd love to encourage anyone struggling to find a support network, they don't even have to be working through the same challenges as you or even be in the same country. Find people who share your values and have hearts of gold. Be open to finding them and take hold of opportunities. You never know what will happen. I have an amazing group of ladies, who I've so far (we have big plans!) only met online through a group programme and mastermind we embarked on together. When I'm having a wobble, need advice or have a win to share they're there for me every step of the way. We have a very special bond and connection and I love them all to bits.

There are so many Facebook groups out there where you can connect with others, be part of a beautiful community and learn ways to help yourself. My absolute favourite for anxiety and stress relief is run by a lovely friend of mine, *The Stress Less Lounge with Elyssa Smith*. I used to struggle with the frustration of not understanding why I was feeling like I was, why I was reacting in certain ways and I hated why my anxiety seemed so illogical. Elyssa has helped me to understand it and has also given me tools to alleviate my anxiety, and general life stress.

My favourite item on my desk is my giant confidence jar. I write in positive words, messages and comments from others, as proof to myself that I am valued, appreciated and loved.

Implementing stronger personal boundaries has been empowering. I can say no when I need to. If something or someone isn't good for me then I'll create a healthy distance to protect myself. I no longer feel that I "should" do something, if I feel I need to protect myself and my boundaries then I'm strong enough to so say.

When I was ill home was my safe space and it still is now. Today I can happily stay at home for days on end having fun with my boys and pottering around the house and garden and not step foot outside the gate. I don't even notice until I stop and think about when I last left. I'm safe and comfortable at home. I've certainly beaten myself up over this before that I *should* be doing this and that and compared myself to others who are out and about. But as I've been on my journey of reflection and development for the last two years I've become much kinder to myself. I can see what makes me tick and why I do certain things; and I'm happy with that. Acceptance of myself has been incredible empowering.

HOPE

When your anxiety plays a major part in your life and impacts you every day it's hard to see how that can ever change. But I hope that I've helped to demonstrate that life can change.

FREE TO BE ME

The support you may need and the work you'll need to do is going to be different for everyone. Different techniques and methods suit different people. The world is so much smaller now that so much is available online.

I would encourage you to do some research and be open to trying different things to find what works best for you. If you feel like you can't do it alone then please reach out to an expert or professional for additional help and support or find a support network like I have.

Since I started my business and hanging out online I've met some incredible women doing the most amazing work to help others. I have no doubt that there'll be someone out there who specialises in exactly what you need. And it doesn't matter if you're at the opposite ends of the world, so much is possible now!

Just like in my work. Through my products & services I help female entrepreneurs around the world to find ways to enjoy marketing their business online and to sign clients with ease; without sacrificing quality time with their loved ones or their health and well-being.

Because of my journey, both personally and professionally, I have so much understanding and empathy for the challenges my clients face when growing their businesses. I love helping them to move forwards.

Balance is at the heart of everything I do as a *Balanced Social Media Marketing Strategist*.

If you're a fellow female entrepreneur using social media to market your business and dreaming of a work-life balance then I would love to warmly welcome you in to my world.

This chapter is dedicated to my late Poppa, whose love and support is never forgotten.

ABOUT THE AUTHOR

ROXY KING-CLARK

Roxy King-Clark is a Balanced Social Media Marketing Strategist who lives in the Falkland Islands. Roxy specialises in helping female business owners to stop feeling like a slave to social media and to instead find ways to enjoy marketing and to sign clients with ease. She helps them remove the pressure, stress, frustration and overwhelm and replaces it with confidence, enjoyment and empowerment.

Roxy loves to learn. Her latest course of study is to become a certified Menstrual Cycle Coach. She truly believes that when we know how to embrace and heal our menstrual cycles then they can become our superpowers and a powerful business asset.

Before starting her business, *Rox Your Marketing*, Roxy worked in quality management, health & safety and oil logistics. A world away from where she is now. After having her two sons, Spencer and Harrison, in quick succession of one another, #2under2, she needed more flexibility and freedom in her life and so she said goodbye to corporate life and hello to building a freedom business.

For the last 10 years she's run her part-time product-based business where she honed her skills in social media marketing. She's also backed up this practical knowledge with a 1st class Business with Marketing Management Degree, a Professional Diploma in Digital Marketing and a small library of online courses.

Roxy helps clients through group programmes, 1:1 Voxer days, workshops, online bootcamps, courses and digital products. Her ever-growing list of publications include a Menstrual Cycle Journal, 320+ Instagram/Facebook Story Ideas book & planner, Manifestation Journals and notebooks.

You can reach Roxy at:

roxy@roxyourmarketing.com

linktr.ee/roxykingclark

roxyourmarketing.com

facebook.com/rox.your.marketing

instagram.com/roxy.lifeinbalance

5

MY DAUGHTER. MY HEART

VALERIE FRASER

Mom. The word I longed to hear from the time I was about thirteen. It took thirty-one years, many invasive procedures, questions, tears, anger and finally an unconditional love before welcoming our daughter into our lives.

Now at fifty-six, my husband and I have a beautiful twelve-year-old daughter, who is spunky, kindhearted, loves all animals, is loyal to her friends and has a wicked and sharp sense of humour! She is confident, brave and so determined when she sets her mind on something. When she calls me *'Mom'* my heart skips a beat: those three letters, M-O-M, are perfect letters to my ears.

The path to how my husband and I became mom and dad was definitely not a straight line but rather a bumpy road that left us a battered and bruised, but we are beyond grateful that we travelled that road. I would not trade anything along that bumpy road, for if we didn't take one of those bumps, we would not have our beautiful daughter

Through my journey with infertility, IVF and adoption I am more tolerant and understanding of the difficult choices people face when building a family. I no longer ask someone when or if they're having children or if they have children. It is invasive and deeply personal. You don't know if she is struggling with infertility has faced multiple miscarriages or is waiting for that phone call that will change her life - the call saying that a birth mom has chosen her.

I have accepted and am proud of how I came through the struggles to welcome our daughter into our family. We have all faced struggles that test our resilience, and strength. In the words of my wise dad, *"We have to play the cards we are dealt."* Those words could not have been more poignant as I traveled the path of infertility, IVF and adoption.

I question some of the choices I made in my twenties and thirties, however each choice I made was with information I had then; not what I know now. Do you remember decisions you made in your past that taught you valuable lessons? Or maybe it changed the trajectory of your life? I have been asked, *'if you could change past decisions, would you?'* Simply, *No.*

Had I changed any of my past decisions I would not have been blessed with the family I have. *'Are you ashamed of some of the decisions you made in the past?'* Yes. However, I have come to realize and accept that I cannot change my past decisions, but I have learned from each one – good and bad - accepted them and moved forward.

When I got my period, I was devastated! Don't get me wrong I knew it was going to arrive one day, but when it did, I knew I was now a woman. Kind of a big thought for a thirteen-year-old! I always wanted children – of course not then - and assumed that I would in the future, like all the women in my life. In my teenage brain, I thought 25 – 30 would be the perfect age to have kids. But God had different plans for me.

In 2003 I met my husband, Steve and we married in 2005. Before we married, we talked about having kids, and although I wanted four, we decided on two as I felt I was too old to have four – I was thirty-eight. Unfortunately, society puts an optimum age on having children and if you pass that age, you become a *geriatric* mother. For those of you who had children later in life, either by choice or circumstance, you have probably heard the same or similar comments I have heard. *'Wow, I wouldn't' want kids at your age,' 'Is it tough being the oldest parent?' 'Do you get mistaken for the grandma?'* When I used to hear those comments, I was devastated and I thought, *'Will I be able to do the normal mom things with my daughter as she grows older?'* Yes, I can and I do!

We started trying to get pregnant when we were engaged as we both knew that statistically at my age it would be more difficult to conceive. We were enjoying life as a newly engaged couple and then as newlyweds, spending time with friends, being active, and travelling, but weren't getting pregnant. That became our whole focus – getting pregnant.

I was tired of people asking, '*When are you having kids? How many kids do you want? Your biological clock is ticking.*' I was acutely aware time was slipping away from me; I did not need reminders. The words sliced through my heart like a knife. It was reinforcement that I was failing as a wife and as a woman. Each time someone asked about kids, a bit of my self-esteem was chipped away.

If you have ever desperately wanted to become pregnant you know what it is like to track your cycle like you're tracking your Amazon package! Every month I had my period, I was pissed at my body for not working the way it should and for letting me down another month! Pissed I couldn't get pregnant as easily as other women! And pissed that the fun of trying to conceive was no longer fun nor was it romantic. Making love to my husband became a means to an end – a baby!

Every time I saw a pregnant woman, I was happy for them, but deep down I wanted to be the one sharing the news that *we* were pregnant. And honestly, I felt jealous. Jealous they had young eggs. Jealous it seemed effortless for them to conceive. Jealous that they would soon be snuggling their baby. Jealous that one day that baby will call them *mom*. How I yearned to hear that word. My shame at not being able to conceive brought self-doubt and a deep-rooted sadness, that was heavy, even on my best days. Every day that cloud of sadness quietly sat beside me.

There were days I questioned why I was still here. I was a failure. I could not build our family. I couldn't do what women have done for centuries – conceive a child.

I have always had a love/hate relationship with my body and finding out my body could not conceive, I sat firmly in the hate side of my relationship with my body. As I sat with my hate, my mental health was taking a beating. At times I was so immersed in my pain, anger, and self-loathing that I could not see that maybe, just maybe the universe had a greater plan for me – it just wasn't visible to me at that moment.

We let very few people into our private hell, so it was devasting when they thought they were being helpful by saying, *Just go on a vacation. It will relax you and you will get pregnant. I know a friend who tried, acupuncture, meditation etc …..*' I know they all meant well, but all I wanted to yell was, '*Shut UP, you have ZERO idea what we are struggling with!*' But of course, I smiled and said, *Not sure, we are just enjoying our time together.* That was a big bag of bullshit! Were we enjoying life as newlyweds, yes, but we were also struggling through anger, pain, and doubt at not being able to conceive.

As people continued to ask us about having children, I desperately tried to hold onto my mental health, but I felt I was losing my grip. There were many dark days that I struggled to get through and when the day was finally over, I dreaded the next day.

After 1.5 years of not being able to conceive we knew something was wrong. We wondered, was my husband sterile, or was I infertile. Not something a couple wants to talk about after less than two years of marriage. But there we were, talking about infertility. Neither of us knew the first thing about infertility. We grew up in families that never talked about anything to do with sex, let alone fertility struggles. We took the first step to find out if my husband was sterile. Nope. All good in that area. I felt there was a neon sign above my head, screaming FAILURE, LOSER! I felt deflated. It was my fault we couldn't get pregnant. I was shattered. Infertility was now a part of both my husband and I and we had to accept it and take the next step. The step into the unknown.

It took Steve and I time to come to terms with the fact we were not going to conceive naturally, so we made the decision to explore IVF. When we embarked on the IVF journey – and boy was it a journey – a lonely journey. Nobody can fully understand the emotional and physical toll of IVF unless they have traveled the same journey. When we shared with friends and family that I was infertile and would be going through IVF, they had no idea what to say. But really what could they say? They couldn't offer advice, nor could they understand the deep pain of infertility.

I knew Steve and I were on our own. Starting this journey without a road map or Google to guide us. The path was strewn with sadness, frustration, hopelessness, anger, jealousy, shame, and anxiety, oh so much anxiety. Would it hurt?

What kind of drugs would I have to take? How much would it cost? So many questions with very few answers. After seeing my family doctor, she sent me to a fertility clinic in Calgary. I never thought I would have to visit a fertility clinic. It was not part of our plan to start a family.

As I sat in the waiting room looking around, I knew that all the women around me were struggling with infertility, experienced self-doubt, cried when they got their periods and were inconsolable when that round of IVF failed. They may have experienced multiple miscarriages and were on round two or three of fertility treatments. I felt their pain. I felt their desire to have a child. I didn't know any of those women, but I felt a sense of sisterhood with them. We were all in the IVF club. The club none of us asked to join.

For those of you who have never experienced IVF, let me tell you it is very clinical and matter of fact. No grey areas, just black and white. The next step on the IVF journey included blood tests, urine tests, delving into my sisters', mother's and even my grandmother's medical history. It quickly became apparent I knew precious little on my sisters', mom and grandmother's reproductive system. It was just something that I never thought to ask my sisters or my mom, let alone my grandmother. As I continued with the tests and endless questions, I knew that my reproductive system was no longer mine, it was soon going to be in the hands of science. No longer mother nature, just pure science.

After the endless rounds of medical tests to determine if I was a good candidate for IVF, we met with the doctor. FUCK. I was a failure once again!

I had an unusually low egg count and for the cherry on top, I was perimenopause. Are you kidding me? I went numb. I was stunned. The voices sounded like the parents' voices in a Charlie Brown show. I am not sure how long I sat there, stunned, but I remember asking him, *'can we still go through with IVF?'* I remember his exact words, *'You can, but I don't recommend it. You have about a 2% chance of conceiving, and the financial cost is quite high.'* For real?

The signs of being a failure kept being thrown at me. Have you ever been so shocked by something you just can't form any words, let alone a sentence? I remember the doctor giving us stats on women who had gotten pregnant with the same odds as me – it wasn't reassuring. He explained that we may want to consider egg donation or adoption as our odds of conceiving with, as I called them my "old" eggs and being perimenopausal were low. The doctor left the room and suggested Steve and I discuss how we wanted to move forward.

This decision would change the rest of our lives. I was 100% sure that I wanted to try. I didn't care about the drugs, or the price – about $12,000. Steve and I wanted to be parents with every fibre of our being. We weren't ready to explore egg donation or adoption - yet. Steve was concerned about all the drugs I would have to take. He was fully aware that I would be taking all the risk, both physically and emotionally, the impact the drugs would take on me. I reassured him I was ok with taking the drugs and the affect they may have on my body and mental health. Little did I know the magnitude that the process would take on my mental health. We agreed we would move forward to Step two.

We took one of the biggest leaps of faith either of us have ever taken. We wanted to take this one shot. We wanted a baby. Even with the odds against us, we decided to move forward with IVF.

The doctor explained there would be needles, lots of them. Oh yes, there were lots of needles. I had to inject myself with two different drugs – twice a day – at the same time each day. The hormone drugs were to help stimulate my ovaries with the goal of creating a viable egg. I had to inject one needle in the stomach and one on my thigh. I remember after a couple of weeks of fertility treatment and continuous needle poking, my mental health was fragile and the pressure to have the drugs work was over whelming. I remember sitting on the edge of our bed sobbing uncontrollably, physically not being able to inject one more needle in my stomach. I told Steve I couldn't do it anymore; I couldn't inject myself with one more needle.

My stomach looked like I had gone five rounds with a prized fighter; it was a maze of bruises from the needles, my legs had track marks like an addict. I asked Steve to inject the needle into my stomach as I cried, asking the Universe to please let this be successful. After Steve had injected me with the needle, I curled up in a ball on the bed and just cried. Steve tried to console me, but I was inconsolable. I turned away from Steve and cried about the pain. Cried that I didn't have anyone to talk to about IVF, to ask if it was normal to be angry, sad, and jealous in the span of five minutes. I wanted to be reassured that the mental and physical pain I was feeling was normal. I longed to talk with someone who had taken the same path as we were taking. As I cried, I knew that these drugs were giving us a chance build our family– a 2% chance but a chance none the less.

Can you remember at time you felt helpless and hopeless and there was no one you could turn to for advice and comfort? It is dark place to experience.

Until we began our journey, we did not realize how cloaked in shame infertility and IVF treatment is. I felt shame for being infertile, shame for having to seek medical help to conceive, and shame for feeling angry at women who didn't need medical intervention to conceive. We didn't share the pain, shame and doubts we experienced with family and friends. How do you explain to them the fear, anger, jealousy, pain, doubt, self loathing that comes with IVF? Simply, you can't. There was little information on IVF at that time. There were no virtual support groups on Facebook and Instagram. I found it difficult to find any support group at all. Steve and I would have to try and navigate this as a team and hope we came out of the journey in one piece and still a couple.

The IVF process is invasive both physically and emotionally. Physically it is the pain of the needles, and the body changes. Emotionally it was nothing I have ever experienced. One minute I was excited at the possibility of bringing a new life into our family and the next I was sobbing uncontrollably, feeling ashamed, and then feeling guilty for feeling the shame. There were days I wanted to run away, hide from everyone. Other days I thought of taking my own life. I was a failure and the loneliness of IVF was so overwhelming. But on the outside, I firmly attached my happy mask.

After three weeks of hormone treatment, we were taking step three on our journey to build our family. Were the drugs enough to produce at least one viable egg or maybe more? The waiting was torture. It was like being in a dream where the clock goes backwards! Finally, we got the call! After all the drugs, tears, doubts and fears I had one viable egg! That is all I needed to hear. One. I was so thankful for science! With the one lonely egg we really only had one chance. This was it. If this failed. . . .don't go there I told myself. Stay positive.

My viable egg was extracted, put it in a petri dish fertilized with Steve's sperm. And we waited. We had success! After about five days we went back to the clinic where the embryo was then transferred into my uterus. As I was lying on the table looking at my Steve, I was thinking nine months and we will have a baby. This could be it!

In three to four weeks, we would have an answer. Positive or negative, those two words would change the trajectory of our lives. When we came out of the room, I was convinced I was pregnant. After two weeks I thought I could see a change in my tummy. I started counting out forty weeks till we would meet our baby. I started to cradle my still flat belly, willing a bump to show up.

When it was time to pee on a stick, I honestly felt I was pregnant. Negative! It was negative. I had Steve go back for another pregnancy kit. After all, it was possible to get a false negative. I was hoping I was one those people. Negative again! I failed again! I remember sitting on the bathroom floor with Steve holding me while I sobbed. I was mourning the loss of having a family. Mourning the loss of a baby my body refused to create. The tears would not stop.

I refused to talk about the failed IVF with Steve. I turned away from him, not for anything he had done but because I was the failure in our desire to build a family. He was 100% able to produce children but because of me we could not. I hid behind my shame and self-loathing. I retreated into myself and shut down. If I could go back to that time, I would be gentler with Steve. Afterall it was not just me that experienced the loss, it was us that experienced the loss. I know Steve was grieving as well, but I was so consumed with my pain, I forgot about his pain.

As the months went by, we experienced the cycle of grief that is felt after a loss, denial, anger, bargaining, depression and finally acceptance. I believe we each travelled through the grief cycle at our own pace and organically we both arrived at acceptance at the same time. We accepted that IVF did not work for us, but that did not mean we could not build a family. We accepted that I will never carry our baby for nine months, never feel them kicking my tummy and there would be no gender reveal party. We accepted our mutual loss and the pain we experienced as a couple, and we agreed to move forward on our journey to parenthood.

Once we acknowledged the fact that we were not destined to have biological children, we realized that it didn't matter if our child didn't have our DNA, nor would they leave a genetic footprint into the next generation. We didn't care if our child didn't have my green eyes and Steve athleticism. Was dark like Steve or fair like me. We realized what mattered to us was bringing "our" child or children into our family and loving them unconditionally. We knew that sharing DNA was not the only way to build a family; love is what builds a family's foundation. We decided to build our family through adoption. We were going to become *mom* and *dad*. As we braced ourselves for the next journey, we didn't know it was going to be emotional and as invasive as IVF.

We entered another world we knew very little about. Although both Steve and my mom were adopted - both were adoptions within the family, we had no clue there were so many ways to adopt a child. Foster-to-adopt, domestic adoption, international adoption, closed adoption and open adoption. So much to absorb.

We agreed it was important to us that we enter into an open adoption plan for a few reasons. Firstly, we would have some medical information and secondly, we wanted our daughter to know who her birth mom was so when the day arrived that she asks about her birth mom, we would be able to provide her with information. Without a doubt it would be hard if/when that day came.

When I think about her meeting her birth mom one day, my stomach drops like it does on a rollercoaster. What if she wants to live with her birth mom? What is she wishes we hadn't adopted her? What if she has a stronger connection with her birth mom than me? So many questions still linger in the back of mind, and I know they will never go away.

We contacted an adoption agency to let them know we would like to build our family through adoption. We were invited to attend a weekend session on adoption where they would answer as many questions as they could. I cried endlessly over the weekend. I am sure I went through two boxes of tissue. Listening to birth moms, adoptive parents and their children was both heartbreaking and inspiring. Heartbreaking because of the young age (eleven) when one of the birth moms became pregnant. Inspiring because we saw the connection between the birth mom and adoptive. The connection of the common love for the baby. As Steve and I listened to a few other adoption stories, I suddenly felt a surge of panic - *what if I couldn't bond with our baby? What if they resent us for adopting them? What if they have questions, we could not answer? What if I didn't love them like biological parents love their kids?*

So many questions swirling around in my head. Suddenly my hand was up. Through my tears, I asked about not loving an adopted child like a biological child. I was reassured not only by one of the adoptive moms, but also from one of the counsellors that it was perfectly normal to experience that fear, anxiety, doubt prior to adoption. Unfortunately, there is so much on the internet that there is an instant and close bond between parents and their biological children, especially with mothers because of the pregnancy process. What I did learn was the bond formed with an adoptive child is formed through the experiences they have shared together. Every time you feed, change, bathe, hug and kiss your child, you bond.

Over the years with our daughter our bond has become unbreakable, and it continues to grow stronger. I have also come to understand that carrying a child and sharing biological data is not always the foundation of a close, loving relationship. The love between a parent and child (biological or adoptive) comes from the care, respect, and nurturing the parent shows their child.

After learning about adoption, we felt hope, more than we had felt since before we began our journey through infertility and IVF. Adoption felt right and we knew this was path was the one we were meant to be on. We were both excited and nervous as we began the slow process of adoption.

Once again, we kept the adoption private as the things we have heard people say about adoption were unbelievable and clueless! *What if the baby has a learning disability or birth defect, can you give them back? If the birth mom had addictions, it will be passed to the baby. I couldn't love a child that wasn't mine. I don't get why people want to adopt? You never know what you're going to get when you adopt. So, really you're not the baby's real parents.* These comments are cruel and come from a place of complete ignorance about adoption. It was comments like those that made us choose not to share our adoption news.

The process of adoption, like IVF is both invasive and emotional. The first step was to provide the agency with information about us as couple and individually. There were no secrets here! The questions ranged from religion, race, sexual history, medical and mental health history. We had police and vulnerable persons background checks and they delved deep into our financial history. Could we afford a child is what they wanted to know? I was a bit shocked by all the deep and personal questions, but I understood why they were asking. The next question was our plan to keep in touch with the birth mom. We hadn't thought of that. A plan? The counsellor explained that a plan is made between the birth mom and adoptive parents such as how much you will allow them into your life. How often will you keep in touch – send picture once a year, get together for holidays? Deep down I wanted to say *no contact at all*, not because I wanted to cut the birth mom out of our lives, but selfishly I wanted our baby all to ourselves. But I knew that wasn't the answer. We agreed that we would send pictures regularly and she could call us on occasion and would be welcome to send our baby birthday or Christmas gifts.

The next wave of questions included what type of child we were looking to adopt? It seems like such a strange question, doesn't it? We were a bit baffled, so she clarified her question. *Were we open to older children? Newborn? Twins? Triplets? Bi-racial? Non-Caucasian? How much drug or alcohol exposure were we open to? Special needs child?* We were a bit taken back by the questions as we never thought of those questions. We would not discount any child that was chosen to be ours.

We asked many questions. *What if the birth mom changes her mind after we bring baby home?* It has happened but we were reassured that the birth mom has ten days to change her mind. After the ten days the process begins to legally adopt and change the child's birth name.

Once we are chosen when do we meet the birth mom? We would meet the birth mom in person once she decided we were the best choice to be adoptive mom and dad. After that it is up to us and the birth mom as to how much contact we have before baby is born.

Then we asked the toughest question, *how long does it typically take for adoptive parents to be matched with a child?* We were told 1 – 7 years, but it could be sooner. We were shocked by how long we would possibly have to wait, but we chose to continue the journey to build our family.

In 2008 we joined the adoption agency. After creating our book with information about Steve and I, our traditions, extended family as well as a letter to the potential birth mom, we waited. Again. We were used to waiting at this point in our journey to build a family. It just seemed natural at this stage. Waiting became our new normal.

In October 2009, we received THE call from the adoption agency. A birth mom had chosen us, and she wanted to meet us in person. We had a boy! A son. We were ecstatic! We were going to be mom and dad! Twenty-four hours later we received the unthinkable phone call– the birth mom decided not to go through with the adoption. I remember leaning against the counter, crying and slowly sliding down until I was a heap of emotions on the floor. I asked Steve *'why, why is our desire to build a family such a struggle.'* The cloud of sadness returned and took up their usual spot beside me. And it brought friends - anger, jealousy, anxiety, and fear.

We went through Christmas that year with heavy hearts. Christmas is my favorite time of year, but Christmas 2009 was missing its glow and sparkle. We knew we needed a break from everything we had dealt with over the last few years from infertility to IVF to adoption. In January 2010 we decided to book a trip to Mexico to relax and clear our minds. I remember sitting on the beach chair in Mexico, looking at Steve and wondering, *will you ever be called 'dad?' Will I ever be called, 'mom?'* In the back of my mind, I wanted to say, *I am done with waiting, let's pull our names from the adoption agency. I don't know, emotionally if I can face another possibility of a match and have it snatched away,* but I kept the thought to myself. I found out later the same thought went through Steve's mind. I believe we were both too scared to say it out loud because if we did, it would be real, we would not be mom and dad. We would continue to be aunt and uncle. I am so grateful for both our silent thoughts that day that did not take life from our mouths. It is now so clear how that one comment would have changed so many lives.

Three days after returning from Mexico we got a call from the adoption agency that a birth mom had chosen us. This time, our excitement was low key as we did not want to get our hopes up to have them shattered - again.

We looked at each other and started to cry. *We have a girl.* We were hopeful that she would not be snatched away. We were provided with the medical history of the birth mom as well as her reason for choosing adoption. We had twenty-four hours to decide if we wanted to pursue the adoption. We didn't need twenty-four hours, we didn't even need 24 seconds - *Yes, a thousand times over, yes* - we want to meet the birth mom. Two days later we sat in a small meeting room talking about why the birth mom chose adoption. We talked about her life and how she arrived where she was that day. As were talked, she told us the baby was kicking! It was magic to feel our little girl kicking, almost like she was saying hello to us. As I looked at the birth mom, I felt nothing but love and gratitude towards her for choosing us. For choosing a better life for our daughter as she knew she could not provide for her properly. I remember hugging her when we left and thinking, as joyful as this moment was for us, the pain she was feeling was probably just as great. She had made the most unselfish decision. For that I will forever be grateful to her.

As Steve and I were walking back to the car, we were like giddy teenagers! Wow, we were going to be mom and dad. We would have the family we had always wanted and prayed for. We knew our daughter was to be born on February 19th,2010. We laughed that maybe she would be born on Steve's' dads' birthday – February 14th or my moms, February 26th. Nope.

Our daughter was born 2 weeks early on Friday February 5, 2010. We got the phone call at 3:00 am and like any new parent we panicked! As I ran in every direction, I was telling Steve all the things we had to do – call my parents, call work, call my sisters – oh wait we have no baby things yet. No car seat, no bottles, precious little clothing and *wait our house wasn't baby proof yet.*

Steve pulled me in and lead me to the car, as I continued to babble. I remember on the ride up to Calgary I called everyone I could think of. As we pulled into the Foothills hospital parking lot, each step we took was taking us closer to our baby girl. It was the slowest elevator ride, ever. Finally, the elevator doors opened onto the maternity ward. Our daughter, our miracle, our world was behind that door. The next few steps would change our lives forever.

When we saw our girl, Steve and I began to cry. The birth mom was breast feeding our girl and said to us, *'Here she is, your daughter.'* I was overwhelmed with emotions at hearing those words. She lifted our daughter towards us and I realized I was shaking so badly I was afraid to hold her. Steve reached over and held our daughter. She was perfect. She fit perfectly into his arms. She was his and he was hers. I pulled myself together and went over to see our daughter. As Steve held her, I counted her toes and fingers and touched her face. For all that's broken in this world holding my daughter is the only thing that made perfect sense. As we stood as a together as a family, no matter how hard the journey was, at that moment I knew it was all worth it. I knew she was destined to be our daughter, and I was so grateful. Grateful for my low egg count, grateful for my perimenopause, endless needles, and a failed pregnancy test. If none of that had happened, I would not be there knowing that this little baby girl would grow up to call me mom.

Our journey was complete. We were mom and dad. But I was most grateful to the birth mom for the unselfish decision she made to choose adoption for our daughter.

Throughout our journey I struggled with sadness, fear, self-loathing and anxiety. I still have triggers that send me into an unhealthy emotional state, but with the help of a therapist I am able to manage the emotions using different techniques. I have learned to take control of how I feel about my body as we did not have a good relationship over the years. I have learned to accept me for who I am and not what society says

I should be. I have accepted that I did not fail at building a family, I took a different path. I only hope that I show my daughter by example that yes, we all face hurdles along the way, some may crack you, but they will not break you. You will come out stronger and more resilient.

When I look at families now, I wonder, *how did you build your family?* That may be an unusual thought, but when you have struggled to build a family, you are truly interested in how other families are built. Or least I am. Someone may choose not to have children while others choose to have six. Some choose to adopt or have biological children and some families are blended to include stepchildren and half siblings. There is no right or wrong way to build a family, but rather people do what is best for them. Every person travels their own path to parenthood. People make choices with the options they have to choose from, or the options they feel they have to choose from – at that time. We are each travelling our own journey, at our own pace.

What I discovered through our journey is that people shamelessly ask very personal questions. We have been asked if *we feel guilty for having one child.* No, we don't. *Don't you want more kids?* No, we don't. *Do you wish you had a biological child that looks like you and Steve?* This is one we choose not to answer as it is deeply personal and so invasive. The short answer is *no*. The long answer is that yes, we sometimes wonder what our biological child would look like. However, each time I look at our daughter I wonder less. Interesting thing is we have been told many times that she looks like Steve.

There is a Christmas ornament I love to hang every year. A stained-glass blue baby buggy. My mom and dad bought it shortly after we started our IVF journey, with the intention of giving it to us for Christmas that year. They didn't. They waited. When our daughter was about three years old, they gave it to me for Christmas and told me the story behind it. Every year I hang the ornament it is a reminder of how blessed we are to have our daughter and how grateful I am for my mom and dad!

As difficult as our journey was, I do know that I would take that journey again, bumps and hair pin turns included if it meant it would lead us to our daughter. From the time our daughter was born she knew she was adopted; we never hid it from her. It is her story too. When she was younger, we told her that she had two mummies – she grew in her birth mummy's tummy, but she grew in my heart. I may not have given her the gift of life, but life handed us the gift of her.

Having faced infertility, IVF and adoption I understand what a difficult journey each one of those are and how much tougher all three together are. As I look back, I realize that my husband and I dealt with infertility, IVF and adoption on our own as we did not know where to go for help, nor was help offered up. If you are going through infertility, IVF or adoption I would encourage you to find a tribe that has travelled that road and lean on them for emotional support. The emotions you will feel are intense and sometimes scary. Your tribe will hold you when the tears won't stop. They will understand your anger. They will feel your heart break. They will know that fear, intimately. They will be your strength.

Although friends and family want the best for you, they do not know the extent of the raw emotions. Make sure you set boundaries. Be clear you do not want or need endless questioning. Let them know you will provide update on your time. Your emotional bandwidth will tap out if you allow people to cross those boundaries. Suggest to family that rather than ask questions you can't or won't answer, maybe they can take you out on a coffee date if they see you are sad. Or lend their shoulder to cry on after an especially difficult doctor's appointment. Or offer a hug - a hug goes a long way on an especially crappy day. And don't let people's comments get you down. You must make the decisions that are best for you and your family, not what other people think is best. Remember to ask lots of questions of doctors, adoption agencies and other people that have travelled the same road. The amount of information thrown at you can be overwhelming but ask questions, continually. The journey will be tough and some days tougher than others but know you will get through it and arrive at the place you are meant to be.

If you are reading this and are facing the uncertainties of infertility, IVF or adoption know that I am here to listen and help you through your journey. Please reach out to me through my Facebook or Instagram accounts. It is a tough journey and having the emotional support will make the journey less of a mystery. And maybe easier.

ABOUT THE AUTHOR

VALERIE FRASER

Valerie Fraser lives in Medicine Hat, Alberta, Canada is a full-time mom to an amazing 12-year-old and works part-time with an organization that educates students on financial literacy and entrepreneurship. Valerie along with her husband own and operate a home inspection business in Medicine Hat.

Valerie has a journalism degree and has written for many newspapers and magazines until she transitioned into corporate communications. Prior to moving to Medicine Hat, she worked with large organizations in marketing and communications.

Through the journey of infertility, IVF and adoption Valerie knows the toll that journey took on her physical and mental health. Because of that Valerie is on a mission to bring both fertility and mental health struggles out of the dark shadows. Valerie's goal is to build a wraparound support team that is accessible to women travelling the path of infertility, IVF and adoption and the mental health challenges that sometimes arise.

 "It is time we talk openly and honestly about infertility, IVF and adoption so that we can support each other through the darkest days and celebrate the brightest joys."

Valerie enjoys spending time with her family travelling (when we can again) camping in the summer and skiing in the winter. She also enjoys watching any sport her daughter is involved with. Valerie also likes to kick back with a glass of wine (red, please) with friends and family.

Valerie is available to speak about the journey of infertility, IVF and adoption.

You can reach Valerie at:

Email – bamf0205@gmail.com

⎈ facebook.com/valerie.greenfraser
⎈ instagram.com/valerie.greenfraser

6

FIND A JOB YOU LOVE...

ANNIE BENNETT

> *'Find a job you love, and you will never have to work a day in your life'.*

I'm not sure where this quote originates… Confucius? Mark Twain? Winston Churchill? They've all been credited with saying it, but whatever its source, it's rather apt.

You see, I'm sitting here, in my small-but-perfectly-formed office, filled with so much joy and contentment that this is now my life, I can hardly put it into words… though as this is the point of a book it would be churlish of me not to give it a good go.

I wake every morning with a sense of purpose, and seriously can't wait to get to my lovely blue desk (with L shaped shelves, and matching 'executive' chair, no less) to start the day's tasks. My week is so purposeful. I time block and set small goals so that I know at the start of the day what I aim to achieve by the end of it.

And the best part? I am accountable to no-one but myself. If I don't get everything done I don't have to explain it, have reasons ready, or make excuses. If I need to finish at noon because my daughter wants some mum time, then I finish at noon. If I get so engrossed in something that I'm here 'til 9pm, no one is hanging around at the door rattling keys because they need to lock up.

Saying that… yes, of course I am accountable to my clients and customers. Things they need me to do, I get done. And I do them well. But the number of clients I have, and the exact timings and deadline of what I do are self-managed, so I never have to overstretch myself, and am therefore never stressed.

Well, rarely. Seven-tiered wedding cakes can get the heart rate increasing and dealing with website tech can turn the air in my little office blue, but the overall feeling is one of calm.

Of course, it wasn't always like that. Far from it. The reason things are so good now, is that I can look back on what things were like and revel in my new self-employed life. Even when that seven-tier wedding cake is making its presence felt, or the website 'drag and drop' isn't bloomin' well dragging and dropping, I can remember my previous working life, thank myself for the changes I've made, and my contentment floats to the surface again. And usually it's that little burst of positive energy that gives me the boost I need to finish the task.

I come from a family of hard workers. Conscientious, strong work ethic, purposeful. Unfortunately, I chose a profession that placed huge demands, and continues to do so to all still within it. It was a very different profession when I embarked on it over thirty years ago, and this I consider to be the main cause of the poor mental health that I suffered in later years. Though I initially did very well in my career, gaining promotion and becoming a leader, the stress of the position, alongside domestic circumstances, caused so much stress that I became physically unwell. I eventually had to leave a well-paid job and find a new source of income.

All through this time there was an overarching feeling of not being in control. I hated that. I'm a bit of a control freak, though 'freak' is probably too strong a word. I am a natural leader. If I see things need doing, I do them, or delegate. I know my own mind, I know when I'm right, and when I'm wrong I take it on the chin and learn from it. But that feeling of everything happening around me, and having no power to stop it, was completely overwhelming.

My default setting is one of a low self-esteem, which surprises most people I know, as one of my life's passions is performance. Theatre, Shakespeare, musicals, opera, classical concerts, I've done it all. I've been told I have a presence on the stage… and I think that's down to the fact that I genuinely love every second with a heart racing passion, and I have a feeling that's what shines through. I had considered a career on the stage at one time, even auditioned for the Glyndebourne Opera Chorus, but domestic pressures meant that I needed a secure and steady income. Being the bread-winner with a young family, with a mortgage to pay, I had to make sure there was enough in the pot, even though I was quickly realising that the career I found myself in was not where my heart lay. I was constantly looking for alternatives, and I'm overjoyed that I've finally found one.

The conversion from my old life, to the one I am now living, took a few years. Had I had the chance, the knowledge, the push… I may have made the break sooner, in fact I did try, but it's not been until now that everything has been aligned. Circumstances, and the choices that I made over the last three years have led to where I am now.

When leading a less than perfect life, it's easy to fall into the 'regret trap'. I've often looked back at the choices I made in my younger days, and wondered why I did this, that or the other, and wondered how different my life would now be if I'd taken the metaphorical right path instead of the left. But the truth is, had anything been different, or I'd made alternative choices, I probably wouldn't now have the things that make my life so fabulous.

I'm a learner. By that I mean, I soak up information around me, and use it to improve my thinking. Over the years, this has led to me being able to look at situations objectively. Stand 'on the outside' and look in. Even when I was at my lowest, I still had the capacity to see what needing doing… I just didn't always have the strength or motivation to do anything about it, and that was what ultimately led to the lack of control I experienced. I have learnt the importance of treating mistakes and failures as learning opportunities and have used them to help me grow both personally, and professionally.

But it took me years to get to the realisation that it's our own self that drives our successes and failures. Yes, there are obstacles that life throws at us, but it isn't the obstacles themselves that prevent us from thriving. It is our reaction to them. It's how we deal with them that dictates how we will then move on and either grow, or wilt.

When I started my adult life these were things I didn't understand. Personal and professional failures were blamed on others, on fate, on luck, on anything rather than accepting that the cause might have been something I had done or not done. At the same time, my lack of self-esteem also meant an inability to recognise that I was capable of dealing with all these failures, that the failure itself didn't define me.

Over the years, I have delved deep, and learnt a lot about how confidence works. I've learnt that it comes from within, and it has to be independent. Yes, it's nice to have close family and friends to support you and make positive noises to boost you when things aren't going great, but unless you are able to stand on your own two feet and know your worth, there's no value in relying on those around you to do it for you. After all, if you believe what is said positively about you, you have to equally believe the negative. It's both or neither. So, having an independent confidence will allow you to hear what is said about you, and you can choose whether to agree or not, without emotions getting in the way.

Part of me wishes that I'd had that independent confidence when I embarked on my career, but that's a regret trap that I'm determined not to fall into. Instead, I shall tell you all about it, and if you can learn something from my experience, spot any warning signs or triggers you might be experiencing, and then make the right choices to deal with them, then, well, my work is done.

I suppose it could be said that I fell into teaching. Both my parents were primary teachers and growing up I was immersed in marking and planning, and the general language of education. I attended schools where my parents had previously worked, so the teachers knew me perhaps a little better than other children in my class. At one stage, when I was about five, I even attended the same school that my mother worked at, though I was never in her class. Other children envied me, thinking I had it easy, but really the opposite was true. My mum never gave me an inch. Not in a mean or unfair way, but I suppose it was a determination not to be seen to be favouring her own that she was perhaps stricter with me than she was of the other children.

Apparently, I was never taught how to read, I just picked up a book and started reading. I take that claim with a pinch of salt, but I suppose having two older brothers in an education heavy household, some things were bound to rub off. I was quick at picking things up, knowing all my tables with lightning reaction by the age of six. I'm told I had an IQ test that came out quite high, so I think sights were set high for me. I had a knack for maths, my brain was, and still is, quite logical, though A level maths defeated me, as I couldn't see the point. My brain needs to know something's purpose I suppose, and I couldn't ever see one for hyperbolic functions.

I'm not telling you all this to impress. If I was going to attempt that I'd describe my ability to solve a Rubik's cube or sing soprano… no, the reason I'm telling you this is to show you how expectations of me were high. I was 'clever', 'bright', 'top of the class'… so a part of me thought that was enough. I never had to work hard to be above where most of the other children were. Knowing what I know now, had I never been labelled with those titles, and been made to earn my place at the dizzy heights I was placed at, I may well have learnt a determination to succeed. I may have developed perseverance and resilience needed to pursue my first passion, performance. Instead, I settled for a career which wouldn't involve a struggle. Primary teaching.

I went straight into university from school, then out of university into my first teaching job. In total, I have spent altogether fifty-two years in education… either receiving it or delivering it. And apart from the holiday office jobs whilst teacher training, and the occasional paid singing gig, until I set up my business I never had first hand experience of any other profession. I suppose there was some sort of security in teaching too, not just financially… but I had been brought up surrounded by it, so knew it from the inside. It was comfortable, I wouldn't need to make much effort to under-stand how it 'ticked'.

My teacher training happened to coincide with the birth of the National Curriculum in the late 1980s. My degree course was full of child centred 'go with the flow' theories, providing 'child centred' education, creating 'whole' children... which was fairly useless in the face of the new curriculum that my contemporaries and I were all faced with the minute we started our first jobs. New teachers in those days had very little support, were just left to get on with the job, unlike the thorough grilling they have to go through these days. We were, on the whole, left to our own devices. I spent the first few years of my career realising that my teacher training had not prepared me at all for the changes I was having to imple-ment, with a definite feeling of not being in control a lot of the time. Not of the children, my height and presence meant I was able to control even the more challenging children. But I made so many mistakes, and the stress was due to me not accepting responsibility for them. Had I known then what I know now, mistakes would have been relished, allowing me to grow. But then, if they had, would I be where I am now? Probably not.

Years went by. Ten years were spent in a very challenging school. I learnt how to create relationships with difficult chil-dren and their parents, I gained a reputation for being firm but fair. I would produce Christmas plays that involved over 100 children, writing them specially for children who found reading challenging. Every child that wanted a line got one, every child that wanted to sing, sang. I provided valuable life experiences for children whose domestic circumstances often left me open mouthed in their complexity. I learnt the real value of education. The real value of a school and the community it can create.

One thing I never wanted at that point though, was promotion. The senior management at that school were dealt more than their fair share of crises, and that was something I didn't want to have any part of. Until I moved to a new school setting. Having been in the same school for ten years, I had become insular. Moving to a new setting made me realise that things could be done in a different way. Rather than lurching from problem to problem, crisis to crisis, challenges were dealt with strategy rather than knee jerk reaction. Staff were encouraged to flourish.

I remember one particular lunchtime, about ten of us were sat eating lunch. The deputy head was talking to one of the senior teachers about a new qualification that was aimed at creating new headteachers. I was taken greatly aback when the deputy turned to me and said *'You should do this. You'd be good at it'*. Up until that point it was a career path that I'd actively turned away from, but it only took that one person's faith in my abilities to turn everything on its head. So, long story short, I trained to be a headteacher.

It was also during this time that my then husband and I started a family. After a bit of a struggle, we finally had two daughters, three years apart. On the face of it, things were good. My career was blossoming, I had a marriage, a family, a house of my own. We moved to a neighbouring county when I was appointed as a deputy headteacher, found schools for our daughters and things seemed to be going well. A few years along the line I became a headteacher, but a few years into that was when things started to unravel.

Looking back, it's plain to see that I was stressed - both professionally and domestically. For various reasons, my marriage was failing, but I couldn't face dealing with that whilst my career was so demanding of my time. It was my job that brought in all the family income. A lot depended in it, mortgage, loans, a few debts, and this coincided with a massive hike in living costs in the late 2000s. My need to be in total control, alongside the massive burdens that I was placing on myself, it's not surprising that something was going to break. And break it did, in style.

Things came to a head in 2012. I had at that point been a headteacher for three years, and taken the school through a successful school inspection. But it was during that year that my domestic circumstances started to unravel. My daughters were primary age, but it felt like I never saw them due to my workload. My failed marriage by then had meant a sale of the family home, and a move to a smaller house, which in itself wasn't a problem, but it was part of the general upheaval. Then in October 2012 came the straw that broke the camel's back.

I remember vividly. It was a Sunday evening. I had been working for most of the weekend, as there was to be an important governors' meeting on the Monday evening. Papers were prepared, emailed out, presentations were ready… but late Sunday afternoon I started to feel unwell. I went to bed early to shake it off, but by the evening I had the hot/cold shivers, inability to move and a temperature of 103. It was full on, proper, not-a-bad-cold, flu.

Now, if you've ever been, or are now, a manager you'll understand my reluctance to postpone the Monday meeting, even if you aren't I'm guessing you've been in a similar situation, others relying on you to produce 'the goods', thinking you'll let lots of people down if you don't show? Well, I was determined that I was going to be there. Or rather, I was determined until about 9pm that Sunday evening, when I found myself unable to get out of bed because my legs were shaking so violently. Realising I was beaten, I called the school's secretary and explained what was happening. She took control, told me to stay where I was and get better, and she would sort out the postponement of the meeting.

I spent the following three days in bed with a high temperature. Couldn't eat, forced myself to drink, slept, shivered, slept, worried… Every day I was determined to be in work the next day, but in the end I had to give in, and signed myself off for the week. Now, as a headteacher, having an afternoon out of school often involved a deal of catching up upon return… so my recovery was impeded by the knowledge that there would be a whole week's worth of issues, both positive and negative, to deal with when I got back, so leaving it longer than a week was not an option.

I attempted to return the following Monday... lasted until 10.30am, then was promptly sent home, and was not going to put up a fight. I was exhausted and still quite unwell. At this point the memory becomes a little hazy... but the upshot was that I developed pneumonia and ended up being absent until the end of December. Over two months absence.

The months that followed involved weeks of staggered returns, relapses and weeks of absence, more staggered returns and more absences. There were situations happening at the school that an 'on top of it all' headteacher would find a challenge, so I found myself, at times, completely over-whelmed by it all. The more I tried to get on top of the catch up, and take control of some difficult situations, the more I struggled. I knew things were unravelling, both professionally and domestically, but I hadn't the strength to stand back and take pause... to see what needed doing... to take stock. I was terrified that the only answer was to leave that job, and with it the financial security it brought. I had no idea what I was going to do, but I didn't want to give up. I didn't want to give in to all the *nay-sayers* who, by that point, were making life very difficult. I did not want to give in.

Then came the second straw for that poor camel. By the September of 2013, I had resolved to return to my work, and attempt to sort through the mess that had been made by my illness and subsequent absences. To say there was hostility in the workplace towards me is perhaps putting it mildly, but I wanted to put things right. As I was by now a single parent, I was finding it very difficult to be a good mum, and it was one particular morning, when everything was happening at once, that I suddenly realised that actually, I don't have to do this. I don't have to prove myself to anyone. I don't have to 'show them'. My health, both mental and physical, and that of my daughters' was far more important than proving my professional worth. So I gave in. I told them I would go.

You will often hear me say that determination, perseverance and resilience are the three words that lead to success. Some might say that it was my lack of determination that led to me giving up that job. For a while I believed that myself. It took months of soul searching and regret to allow myself to stand tall again. But looking back, I did have a determination. Not the obvious one of keeping my job. Rather, I was determined that my health, and that of my children would no longer suffer. There was a determination 'switch'. The realisation that the path that was being taken, the path that was seen by many as the only alternative, wasn't the path that I should continue along. My new determination was to find a new path.

In the months that followed I had some time to consider my options. Although terrified at the prospect of potential financial insecurity, I was overwhelmed with excitement that this, finally, was the chance I had to do something new. By this point, the draw of performance and the stage was less strong.

I still sang, and with the group that I was a part of, I sang leading roles, and that was enough for me. I couldn't see myself giving that up to stand at the back of a chorus, however much I'd be paid for it. So, I looked to my skills to find a new income. I decided that it would be a baking business, with the longer term aim of making wedding cakes.

So, *Leading Lady Cakes* was born. To start with, for financial reasons, I needed to build my business alongside working as a supply teacher, which worked well, allowing me time to develop my skills and build my business. I wasn't without doubts though… I did go back into the classroom full time for a short while when money became tight, and to 'get back on the horse'… but I quickly realised any heart I had in that profession had long disappeared, so I made the break from full time work, and moved back into supply work, determined to build my business even further.

It was March 2020 when things took yet another dramatic turn. I had built my business, was getting more and more wedding cake enquiries and bookings, had a number of weddings in my diary for that year, and was teaching a few days supply to just boost the income.

But, over the course of one evening, late March, I not only lost those bookings, but also the supply teaching work all in one go. Covid had arrived.

However, by this point, I had strength. I wasn't prepared to throw in the towel. I was determined, resilient and ready to persevere and do what it took to keep going. My saving grace was the power of networking. By that point, I was a member of a number of online wedding industry groups, and when covid hit, the industry quickly fell into crisis. Many of the networking groups offered support and help to businesses affected, and it was during one of those online conferences that I came across something that had not been part of my world up to that point. The concept of the 'business pivot'.

This was really a game changer. Knowing that I wouldn't be getting any income from neither wedding cake making, nor the fall back of supply teaching, I realised that through a 'pivot' I could change my business model and create opportunities for other sources of income. I had skills that I could share with others, that were worth something to others. So, with the help of some wonderful online training, I set up *Annie Bennett Business*, with the aim of helping hobby bakers set up their own home baking businesses.

During the months of 2020,I set up my second website, www.anniebennett.co.uk I set up an online Facebook group, The Home Baking Business Community UK, which grew really quickly. I created courses, which people bought. I wrote books, which people bought. I set up a membership, The Home Baking Professionals Society, that people subscribed to. All this income came in because I was taught how to use my skills, to grow an audience, and then share my skills with that audience, both gratis and for a fee.

Interestingly, my input in my Facebook group, which as I write this has just over seven thousand members, isn't predominantly cake based. I find myself talking more about business positivity and attitude than I do about making cakes. My main message to those in my online groups, and those that I support in setting up their own home baking businesses, is that there are no failures. Mistakes are not to be avoided at all costs. If I have learnt anything in my 30 odd years as an adult, it's that we can't avoid getting things wrong. We can't avoid making wrong choices. We can't look into the future and decide which path is best, because the one we choose isn't always going to be the one that ultimately benefits us.

But, mistakes are there for a reason.

Imagine a baby when they are learning to walk. On their first attempt, on those chubby, wobbly, unsteady legs, the chances of them falling is high.

Do they stop?

Do they think *'Well, sod this for a bunch of soldiers, I'm not built for walking. I'll just get mum to carry me around for the rest of my life'…?*

Do they lie on the floor waiting for assistance because they have given up?

No, of course they don't. They don't have the life experience to make those choices. Their instinctive, caveman brain is telling them to get up and learn how to do it, because they might be in danger if they don't. Their brain is telling them what to change each time they have a go… let's try with a leg here, or an arm here, that might work better… all the time

they are experiencing trial and error, until they get it right...
and even then, it takes a lot of practice to go from that to
running, hopping, skipping and galloping. If adults applied
that resilience to new situations, rather than assuming they
can't and giving up, we would have many more happy workers, business owners, performers and people doing what they
love.

If I was a believer in forces beyond our control I might say
that the planets had aligned at the perfect time, giving me
the opportunity to break away from one profession and
establish myself in another. But the thought of allowing any
phenomenon, natural or otherwise, to take control over my
life is one I'm not ever likely to entertain. I truly believe that
we are a result of the choices we make, and of our reaction
to those things that happen around us. These days, I rarely
wish people good luck. You're far more likely to hear me say
'go for it'. Placing reliance in 'luck' is akin to negating the
responsibility we have to ourselves. Success comes as a direct
result of the effort that is put into the gaining of it. It's a
fairly well known theory that an Olympic gold medal is won
by practising for 10,000 hours. Having an aptitude for a
sport or skill is not enough to take you to the top. You need
that dedication, and if you have passion then the dedication
will come so very easily.

I found I had a passion not only for creating beautiful cakes,
but helping others do the same. Having someone tell me that
one of my live sessions, or training guides, or even just a
reply to a question, has helped them to set up their own busi-

ness, just fills my heart with utter joy. Knowing that I've guided with the right information, and convinced them that anything is possible, and to learn from their mistakes really is one of the reasons that getting up in the morning is such a joy. *'Who might I help today?'*

If you have the passion to succeed, then you will do so through determination, perseverance and resilience.

Luck will have very little to do with it.

Find a job that you love…

ABOUT THE AUTHOR

Annie Bennett, *The Home Baking Business Specialist* is a baker, author and teacher who helps home bakers to set up home baking businesses.

Before she started her own wedding cake business, *Leading Lady Cakes*, Annie was a primary teacher and headteacher for over 30 years, and not only taught thousands of primary age children, but mentored many fledging teachers, working with local universities to help start many teaching careers.

She decided to make the break from primary education in 2014 to set up *Leading Lady Cakes*. Taking her mentoring skills into the baking world in 2020 she set up *Annie Bennett Business*, and now helps fledging bakers to set up on their own.

Annie is a fully trained operatic soprano, hence the name of her baking business. She has also appeared in semi and non-professional theatrical productions (never call her am-dram dahling!) including many musicals and Shakespeare. Her Titania was a wonder to behold.

Annie has a free Facebook group, the Home Baking Business Community UK, a membership, the Home Baking professionals Society, and many courses available, which are priced to enable easy access for start up businesses. She is also available for 1:1 consultations.

You can reach Annie at

Email: admin@anniebennett.co.uk

Website: https://anniebennett.co.uk/

YouTube:

https://www.youtube.com/c/AnnieBennettHomeBakingBusinessSpecialist

Her chapter in this book is dedicated to her parents and her daughters, whose support during the low times made the mountain so much easier to climb.

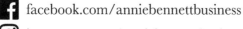 facebook.com/anniebennettbusiness
instagram.com/anniebennettbusiness

7

THE LOTUS

LAURA ROWE

*T*here is a light, almost effortless feeling of freedom within my heart. I am no longer tied to anything or anyone that does not bring me joy. I choose me, every single time, guilt free. No more feeling selfish for putting my needs first. I am in full bloom, but I certainly never used to feel this way.

Snapping at my son when I felt tired, and feelings of despair when things didn't go to plan. Sound familiar? We're human, it happens. The difference is, now I recognise those emotions creeping to the surface. I can accept I need to move through those feelings, and when it's time, I let them go. Surrendering to my needs without judgement, is key. Tears, anger, upset, they all serve a purpose. 'You've got to feel it to heal it' is a quote that I always remind myself of in difficult times, and it's so true. Emotions give you the permission to process, to release, to understand your next move. With practice, I am now better able to respond, rather than react to situations, with a much clearer mindset. And it's liberating!

I have never felt more in control, aligned, and trusting that I am on my true path, as I do today. I'm living my passion and it makes me feel alive with purpose. I am the healthiest version of myself that I have ever been. I have passion, and so much love and kindness for the person I am today. And I get to help others, on a global scale, step into their light too. My wellness retreats sell out in minutes, my classes are booked up in advance and I show hundreds of people at a time, how they can find calm amongst their chaos, just like I did. I have found my true calling and it feels amazing!

I specialise in bespoke mindset programs, transformational healing workshops, luxury self-care retreats and offer an inspiring wellness membership - **This is Modern Holistic Healing!** A place where traditional healing techniques and the modern world align.

Despite living my life today with Fibromyalgia and chronic fatigue, due to the extensive damage long term stress and a lifetime of trauma has caused my body, how can I not, in some way be grateful for the darkness that brought me here? I wouldn't be the person I am today if I hadn't gone through everything I did, exactly the way I did. Everything that has happened in my life wasn't happening to me, it was happening for me. Today, I'm an Author, a Public Speaker, a successful Life Coach and Wellness Advocate. It set me on the path of holistic education and healing that I walk today, living my life in true alignment, and appreciating the need for that balance and harmony we could all use a little more of in our lives.

And if nothing else… we can use my past as an example of *what not to do* when it comes to stress, and how important it is to manage your wellness.

We are all waking up to the fact that we are both hyper connected and disconnected at the same time, and this is having a massive impact on our wellbeing. For me, these words resonate so deeply;

> *"If we don't make time for our wellness, we will be forced to make time for our illness"*

> — JOYCE SUNADA

Either way, we will be forced to make time, right? Absolutely.

I had tunnel vision. I could only see the bad, the worst outcomes. I was that snowball rolling down the side of the mountain, gathering more snow as I went. Only my snow was not the fluffy white powdery stuff you see in adverts, mine was more like the dirty brown slushy stuff everyone tries to avoid.

My life was noisy, chaotic, and fast paced. I cared too much about the opinion of others. Dimming my light so I could fit in and feel accepted by those around me. Desperate for approval and suffocated by societal expectations and external pressures. I'd forgotten how to think for myself.

I was erratic in my behaviour, completely unaware I had become addicted to stress.

I was unhealthy, not just with my physical fitness and the fact I was constantly battling sickness, but my mental health and self-worth was at an all-time low. Life felt dark and heavy, like I was wading through thick mud. I had turned away from the sunlight, unable to bloom, and kept myself in the safety of darkness.

I was self-medicating... alcohol, parties, holidays, boys... Tricking myself into believing I was having a great time. Now, don't get me wrong, I was having a great time... but I was hiding. Sabotaging my own happiness. Hiding from the pain because it was too difficult to deal with and hiding from having to take responsibility in sorting out my life. I needed to get out of my own way, but I couldn't.

I hid behind a mask every single day, looking healthy and well on the outside, always laughing and full of smiles, but on the inside, it was a toxic environment, and the total opposite of the person I was portraying to the world.

I had lost faith that things would ever feel any different. But when I look back, I guess there was always a small part of me that did believe. A part that knew I was living other people's lives, that knew I needed to step away from it all and find my own path. It's hard coming to that realisation, scary hard in fact. Especially for the people pleaser that I was then. But I always tried to remind myself that nothing changes if nothing changes. And the fact was, I was anxious, depressed, and miserable.

I wish I'd known back then that holding onto that little spark of faith that things would get better, was all I needed. That spark was going to grow, and eventually ignite that fire within me that burns so bright and passionately today. It was the true me burning to get out, desperate for change, and waiting patiently for her turn. Waiting until she just couldn't wait any longer and needed to take matters into her own hands. Enough was enough.

My inner fire is my intuition, my inner knowing, my gut feeling. She guides me and I trust her (we've been through a lot together). She taught me to take a leap of faith, even when I felt hesitant. She taught me to believe that the universe would always catch me. Even if I didn't know where I was going to land. If I lean into my intuition and trust the timing is right, the rest will fall into place. We are always exactly where we are supposed to be. Everything that happens is preparing us for the next stage of our life.

I never knew what I wanted to do with my life, or who I wanted to be. And that's ok. I made peace with that, as I stepped out into the big wide world at sixteen, on my path of self-discovery.

I'm an empath and I've always been drawn to helping people. Feeling their pain, carrying their emotions, and wanting to help make it better. And because of this, I found myself attracted to broken men. Men who had problems way beyond my young and naive capabilities, which meant I was the one who ended up needing to be saved. So, I became my own hero. Eventually...

Turbulent relationships, filled with lies and deceit, left me broken for a while. I was hyper vigilant to almost everything; paranoid, anxious, and stressed to the max. Overreacting and snapping were a regular occurrence.

I spent years mentally exhausted. Still with no idea what direction I wanted my life to go in? Existing. Working to pay debts that weren't mine, living in fear of something happening to me or even being kidnapped, and no one would ever know the truth because I kept it all bottled up. I was screening calls and messages, experiencing mystery illnesses, just pushing through to the weekend when I could lose myself in distraction.

I was trapped in other people's broken world's, drug addiction, sex addiction, the need for control, intimidation, isolation, compulsive lies and cheating. I was there, right in the middle, for the most part blissfully ignorant to the fact. And when I began to discover the truth, I felt as though I had been brainwashed. The life I was living was a lie. Why did this keep happening to me?

I guess you'd think this would make me an untrusting person. That's where I tell you that it's not true. I trust completely until proven wrong. I decided early on that I wasn't going to punish anyone for someone else's mistakes. Maybe that's what got me in similar crappy situations three times consecutively? I still live by that rule today, and after spending all these years finding myself, healing myself, setting healthy boundaries, and knowing how to protect my energy, I have happily spent the last ten years in a loving, trusting relationship.

I always had older friends from a young age. I guess this gave me a sense of freedom, a maturity. I gained my confidence and understanding of the world around me from their conversations and experience. This is where comparison really started for me. I was desperate to be liked by my older peers, and not be seen as the baby that I was.

I always dated older men and left home at a young age. Packing my bags, stepping out into the big wide world, believing I knew it all, when in fact I knew nothing.

I lived with, and survived domestic abuse in not one, not two, but three different relationships over the span of twelve years. And those years had a huge impact on my health. A decade of emotional and physical abuse was not good for my body or my soul!

No convictions ever took place because I never spoke about it to anyone. My mouth was sealed shut. Partly denial, partly fear, partly shame and embarrassment, but mostly because I thought I had it handled, playing it down with humour and always making light of situations. I was brainwashed. I had become a master of disguise. Bottling up my feelings, pasting over the cracks and getting on with whatever was thrown my way.

Dealing with this kind of behaviour towards me from such a young age really left me lost as a person for a long time. I felt as though I was existing rather than living, simply surviving rather than thriving in my life.

I was stuck in a pattern of abuse I couldn't see a way out of - external abuse from them and internal abuse that I was causing myself through guilt and denial.

I lived my life in fight or flight, FOR YEARS. I was stuck, negatively reacting to situations rather than logically thinking, and responding in a reasonable way. But I had no idea this was the case at the time. This was my normal. Catastrophizing situations and spiralling out of control in my head.

I was constantly living in fear, worry, upset, or stress. These were my default settings, and this made me a very negative person. I was down on myself, down on the world around me, and 99% of the time, angry with something or someone. But you would never have known. I was always smiling and always laughing. The life and soul of any (and every) party.

It took everything I had in me to leave each of those relationships. Every time losing my possessions, taking with me all I could carry, knowing I would have to build my life again from scratch. I don't know where that strength came from? But something in me just snapped and I no longer felt anything. I was numb and done with it all. That was the moment I knew I could leave. It's a surreal feeling, almost like you are walking in slow motion around muffled chaos… you feel nothing, and you hear nothing. I knew I was better than this and I deserved more for my life. I dug deep and I found my brave, every single time. Out of that darkness, that thick heavy mud, a lotus flower was starting her bloom.

Years of negative self-talk, believing I deserved the life I'd been dealt meant I struggled with any kind of pressure. I couldn't hold down jobs long term because I couldn't handle more pressure in my life. I was feeling lost and unfulfilled. I didn't know what to do with my life, I didn't know who I was in this life? My stress container was full to bursting and I had lost the valve release key to ease the pressure.

It always felt like I was rushing around from one place to another, relying on my stress addiction as a level of comfort. I know it was an avoidance tactic, keeping me from dealing with my emotions. Keeping busy meant I could avoid dealing with those deep and painful layers of loss, grief and anger that had built up over those 12 years. I had become a master avoider!

I built up walls of steel around my heart. I became hard, closed off, and some might say, an ice queen. I was emanating way too much masculine energy. But I had convinced myself I needed to be this way to survive, to stay protected and in control.

I was always unwell with one thing or another, my health was suffering. My body wasn't nourished, my mind was in overdrive and my immune system was low. If there was a cough or cold, I caught it. I had eczema all over my body, my hair was weak and falling out, I regularly had neuralgia, migraines, allergies, and suffered with IBS symptoms. You name it, and I was experiencing it. It felt like even my body was against me.

I had no idea my mental health was affecting my physical wellness in such a dramatic way - it was all connected. I was completely uneducated in the world of self-care, never thinking my own mind could make me so unwell.

I was totally unaware that I was living with anxiety and depression. I had heard about them, but I didn't know what symptoms to look out for. I knew I was feeling low, but I was content there. I thought it was just who I was? That's the problem with spending all that time alone, in your own head, you start to agree with your own terrible advice. I'm sure we can all relate to this.

I stopped looking after myself completely for a while. I couldn't sleep at night, and I couldn't wake of a day, I wasn't eating properly, I stopped caring about what I was wearing, I would avoid answering the phone and seeing friends, and would cancel plans and appointments at the very last minute. Working became almost impossible as I became more and more withdrawn.

I was stressed, depressed, broken, and lost.

Even for years after these relationships had ended, I continued with these self-destructive patterns of behaviour, because I knew nothing else.

It wasn't until I was diagnosed in 2016 with thyroid cancer, did I sit up tall in my seat. "Say that again?"

FUCK.

I found a lump in my neck whilst in the middle of the Balearic Islands with my partner. The beauty of the island, the light and carefree sensation of being on holiday, the bright, light of the sun's rays beating down on my face, all overshadowed by the darkness of uncertainty I was now feeling.

Scans, ultrasounds, bloodwork, endoscopies, and biopsies all came back clear. I was relieved, but I also needed answers. There was an overwhelming stress and unease I just couldn't shake. Countless phone conversations and face to face meetings with consultants and specialists, over weeks and months because I couldn't settle. Everyone telling me I was fine, that there was nothing wrong with me, and the symptoms I was experiencing were just due to worry and stress. But I knew my body, and I was now having to fight to prove there was something not right. More stress and upset on an already stressful and upsetting situation. I slid straight back into default mode… running on stress and adrenaline.

Enough was enough, I wanted this lump taking out and I wasn't taking no for an answer. So, I continued to fight until it was agreed to remove the lump. I was told there were only three reasons they would do the procedure: If it was cancer, which according to them, it wasn't, if it's obstructing my airway, which they said it wasn't (I disagreed), or for cosmetic reasons. At this point the fight was wearing me down, so I agreed to the procedure under cosmetic reasons. I just wanted it out.

A hemithyroidectomy was agreed to remove the mass in my neck, along with the left half of my thyroid.

Waking up in recovery, it was explained to me that the lump they removed had attached itself to the muscle in my neck, which meant part of that muscle also needed to be removed also.

During my follow up appointment, they told me that there was a 1% chance my lump was cancer, and guess what, I was that 1%. I was diagnosed with a Thyroid Papillary carcinoma, left side, stage two.

In that instant, something switched in my brain, and we were no longer talking about me. In the time it took the consultant to tell me my diagnosis, I had completely detached myself from the situation. Compartmentalised – from that moment it wasn't happening to me; we were always talking about another person.

By doing this, it meant telling family and friends was easier because in my head, we weren't talking about me. I was factual and emotionless for the most part. And by not falling apart, it made those around me feel more reassured that everything was going to be okay.

As a precaution, I decided on a second procedure to remove the other half of my thyroid, for fear it may have spread. Eight weeks after a total thyroidectomy I received radioiodine oblation. All of which has left me on thyroid hormone replacement medication for the rest of my life, and a frail body that was no longer recognisable to me. The cancer *had* spread to the other side of my thyroid. I made the right decision.

Recovery was long and slow. During my radioiodine therapy I had to isolate and was unable to be around my son, who was seven at the time. He knew I was sick, but I never told him it was cancer. He thought cancer meant you were going to die, and I wasn't strong enough for that conversation and neither was he. During that quarantine period the closest we could be to each other was me at the top of the stairs and him at the bottom. He didn't understand, and it was heart breaking. So, together we came up with a secret code, a code only we understood. We would leave secret messages for each other around the house, reminding each other of how much we loved and missed each other. The code consisted of shapes, dots, and patterns, taking me forever to decipher, but all I had then was time. When I ask my son, now twelve what he remembers about that time I was sick, he talks about how hard being separated was, but how fun we made it with our own secret code language. I'm so grateful for this being his only memory of that difficult time.

There is no doubt in my mind that receiving my cancer diagnosis was the catalyst that sparked change. I was at rock bottom, lower and sicker than I thought I could ever be. All the low places I had been before turned out to be nothing compared this. But I needed to be healthy, there was no way I was leaving my son without his mother.

I began to research my diagnosis, looking more into understanding cancer, different lifestyles, environmental factors, studying holistic practices, diets, and science backed research. I began educating myself on the connection between chronic stress and physical wellness. I couldn't stop! I became fixated on education as a way of coping with what I was going through. The information I was discovering was shocking to me. I needed to share what I found with anyone that would listen.

This is where my holistic journey became my priority, and ultimately my passion.

It was through this research that it became clear to me that this and all the other health scares I had received over the years were all stress related. My lack of knowledge around healthy stress management had contributed towards all of my illnesses.

What my cancer did for me was give me time. No more rushing from one thing to another. No more avoidance tactics. It forced me to slow down, to pause, to look up and find the sunshine. I had all the time in the world to reflect and I was gifted the chance to choose again.

The pivotal change for me was learning how to find the calm in my chaos. We all carry too much noise around in our heads; mum jobs, mum guilt, work, external opinions, expectations, criticism, judgement, self-doubt, the list goes on... So, learning how to filter through those thoughts and manage them in a calming way was a game changer for my journey. I finally cracked it when I discovered meditation. But not sitting, legs crossed, dressed in white, and listening to whale music, kind of meditating. I like to do things my way. So, by combining the things I enjoy (yoga, meditation, intention, science), I was able to settle both my body and my mind with ease and have them working in harmony together.

Understanding the energy that I bring to the table, and protecting myself from negative energy brought by others, has played a huge part in my growth. Setting healthy boundaries to support my goals seemed daunting at first, but when we take it one step at a time, and one day at a time, the momentum builds. We start to see subtle changes in mood and mindset for the better. Things no longer feel as heavy as they once did, and we start to feel stronger, more capable, even if we still don't have all the answers. That feeling of inner peace keeps you aligned with the inner knowing that things will work out exactly as they are supposed to. Our reaction towards an action is what gives it meaning or importance, not the action itself.

Keeping myself in a dark and negative space for so long, just like that lotus flower, and moving from a place of anger only brought me more pain. Drinking the poison and expecting your enemy to die, couldn't have rung truer. But I was stuck there, and I blamed myself for staying there, I was trapped in a vicious cycle. Stopping myself from blooming and shining my colours bright.

At the time I needed it the most, The Law of Attraction became my guide. It's the idea that our experiences are created by our thoughts, feelings, and emotions. What we think and the way we feel is what we attract. And I no longer wanted to attract the bad, the negative, the unhappy. Around 80% of what we think is controlled by our subconscious mind. For things to change for the better we need to have greater awareness around what we are thinking, or it makes change difficult.

When it comes to healing the body and the mind, awareness was key in my healing journey, and for this reason it has become a major part of my teachings. As soon as I began to move with mindful awareness with everything I did, my life began to change. Because of this, I created fusion workshops and classes based around my skills and knowledge combined. Teaching others the importance of finding their quiet, to calm the noise with ease, and to begin to move from a place of conscious awareness.

Healthy boundaries were firmly put in place to protect my peace of mind. Toxic relationships and friendships became a thing of the past and it felt good. *"It's important to understand that setting boundaries isn't a way to get rid of people, but a way to keep them in your life without destroying your inner peace"* Vex King.

We need to better understand that our thoughts and emotions carry a vibrational signature that magnetises more of the same. If we feel negative or stressed, we send out negative, stressed-out frequencies, attracting more. Equally if we wish to create a better life for ourselves, the power we give to our thoughts is vital.

I challenge you - each time you catch yourself having a negative thought or emotion, nonjudgmentally and always with kindness, interrupt yourself and change the story you tell yourself.

That conscious act of interrupting negative thoughts, beliefs and emotions will in time help you reprogram more positive thinking patterns in your subconscious mind and help support you on your healing journey.

Something unexpected happened on my healing journey… I fell in love. I had never even considered this before and certainly never said the words 'I love you'… to myself. We are all guilty of this. Have you ever said the words I love you to yourself? Looked into your own eyes in the mirror and said the words? It's certainly not easy for most people, and it took me a few attempts to not feel weird about doing it. But the truth was, that I *was* falling in love with this new person blossoming into existence. She made me proud. My mind felt clearer, my body was healing, and my heart felt happier.

And that is the golden thread that runs through everything I teach today… To love ourselves a little harder, to be gentle to ourselves, the same way we are to others. We rarely show ourselves the same kindness and compassion. And I bet if the outside world could hear half of what we say to ourselves, we would no longer say it. So, I am here to remind you that you are whole and perfect as you are, you have just forgotten, and that's ok, so did I. But once I found courage, confidence, and compassion for myself, I began to open up my heart and blossom into that beautiful lotus flower.

I have helped so many clients over the years find themselves again, using a whole-body mindset. Clients who have gone on to reignite the spart in their marriage, clients with crippling anxiety who have built their own self-care toolkit to support themselves medication free, clients who have made huge career changes and stopped settling for less than they deserved. I have been a lifeline for hundreds of people, worldwide, struggling during a global pandemic, and I have worked in rehabilitation with many clients to help improve mindset and mobility. The best bit? Some loving friendships have been formed too, not just with me, but with each other too, through the wonderful community of likeminded soul's lifting each other up in my free Facebook community that I created during the pandemic as a safe and uplifting space for people to be online.

I am proud of myself and where I am today. Looking back over how far I have come and what I have achieved, despite it all.

I have only been able to come this far by really working on my mindset and choosing to find gratitude in every situation.

It wasn't easy and I didn't always feel like this, but I wouldn't have felt strong enough to have made some of the difficult life decisions I have, without adopting positive mindset practices. They helped me connect to my true self and recognise my worth. This made me want to take care of myself more. And so, combined with my physical practices of yoga, meditation, a balanced diet and exercise, shifts began happening. I was ready to receive, and the universe started to respond. I worked on both my physical and mental wellbeing as a whole entity, bringing back balance. I found that by uniting the two I could not only hear myself again, my true self, with all the noise filtered away, so I knew what direction I was going in, but I also found that I became lighter and freer in my body too. My smile was genuine, my frown removed. I was no longer living my life in regret. Daily affirmations, positive mantras, all reinforced the way I was feeling and the way I wanted to feel. It was contagious.

Each little positive win spurred me on to the next, then the next, then the next, one day at a time.

Now, I'm not saying to be positive is all you need. Plus, easier said than done, right? That would be irresponsible of me. Everyone is different and we all need to work within our own limits and do what is right for us. However, when we start to make small changes in a positive direction, they begin to attract more positive changes as you start to see results. Our vibration raises and matches with the good we wish to receive.

Today I teach many of these combined practices to my clients with phenomenal results.

Through the most traumatic of circumstances, most of which I wouldn't wish on my worst enemies. I have learned to find the positives and reframed my negative thinking patterns to serve me and heal me in the most positive of ways. I quit my stress and took charge of my life.

Myself, my body, and my mind, have been through some dark times. I know how it feels to be incredibly low in your life and believe there is no other option. I understand how it feels to have your mind so full of noise that you lose yourself. And because of this lived experience, I know that there is another way... because I created one. I used my despair as fuel to manoeuvre myself to better things. The resistance and struggle you are experiencing are signs from the universe that you are not on your right path and it's trying to push you in the right direction towards your Dharma (true spiritual path). What is meant for you will always find you. Flowing not forcing is how live my life, and you can too.

Using my time working in neurology and neurosurgery I understand the science of the brain. I know focused breathwork and meditation can start to switch on the relaxation response in the brain, and combining them really packs a punch when it comes to filtering out the noise we carry that doesn't serve us well.

Add to that, gentle yogic movement or stretches to release tension and stagnant energy trapped within the body, and we are starting to really create the perfect environment for mind body coherence. *"This is the state when the heart, mind, and emotions are in energetic alignment and cooperation"* Dr. Rollin McCraty. Resulting in lower blood pressure, heart rate improvement, increase in oxytocin production, and the level of cortisol in our blood lowers, reducing our stress levels and moving us away from that fight or flight response that can really cause serious illness if we spend too much time in that state.

I build bespoke self-care tool kits for all my clients. Working together, we deep dive to the root cause, at a comfortable pace. I'm arming you with the right techniques and practices to help you feel more in control of your racing mind. I can show you how to build a healthy self-care routine into your life with minimal disruption. We are all busy people and looking after ourselves can easily slide to the bottom of the 'to do' list, causing the negative self-talk, that begins that cycle of lack.

For as long as I can remember, I have always been drawn to the beauty of the lotus, even without realising its significance in my life. When I discovered it symbolises healing, self-realisation, self-regeneration, and rebirth, I had them tattooed on my body as a visual reminder that even when the roots may start in the dirtiest of waters, far away from the sun, the lotus soon reaches the light to produce the most beautiful flower. I am the lotus flower. You can be too.

I want to leave you with this short mindset reset exercise that you can refer to whenever you feel your breathing becoming short and shallow, when your heart is beating a little quicker, or your thoughts become overanxious. With practice, you will soon start to feel calm, capable and in control. This became a lifesaver for me on my journey and I wish to gift it to you.

- Sit comfortably, with your back supported and both feet on the ground.
- If your feel safe to do so, you can close your eyes or lower your gaze.
- Begin by feeling into any sensations within your body.
- Tune into your breath. No need to change it, just begin to have an awareness towards the quality of your breathing, non-judgmentally.
- Placing one hand onto your heart centre and one hand to your tummy. Start to become aware of your natural rhythm as you connect your breath with your body. This allows for the creation of space.
- Aim to lengthen your exhales now, as you feel into the flow at a steady pace.
- Now, notice your breaths journey – become aware of how your breath enters your body, how that breath travels around your body, how your body reacts to the breath, and then how the breath exits your body.

- Repeat to yourself: 'I am safe'. 'I am loved'. I am supported'.
- Let yourself take up this space for as long as you need.

You can practice this short reset as many times as you need, to help you come back home to yourself.

ABOUT THE AUTHOR

LAURA ROWE

Laura Rowe is the owner and founder of Align Lifestyle. She is a global Wellness and Empowerment coach, an ex-NHS theatre practitioner, a health science specialist, and a trauma and cancer survivor, on a mission to help people rediscover who they are at their core, to see how truly powerful they are, and to gain emotional freedom by living intentionally and finding calm in the chaos of life. Because after struggling for years with anxiety, depression and eventually cancer,

Laura learnt the hard way, that if we don't make time for our wellness, we'll be forced to make time for our illness.

> *"I am passionate about creating a society with less burnout, anxiety & stress, so we can be a nation more focused on health, wealth & happiness."*

Using science backed holistic modalities such as meditation, breathwork, yoga and mindset practices, Laura is here to help more of us embrace better health without it feeling like a chore.

Laura is the Founder of Align Lifestyle, a certified Yoga and meditation instructor | Yoga and Ayurveda practitioner | Law of attraction Mindset coach.

Laura is available for public speaking events, wellness projects, as well as private consultations.

You can reach Laura at:

Email – hello@alignlifestyle.co.uk

Website – www.alignlifestyle.co.uk

facebook.com/alignlifestyleliverpool

twitter.com/iamlaurarowe

instagram.com/align_lifestyle

linkedin.com/in/laura-rowe-align-lifestyle

8

DON'T JUST RISE, SHINE!

JO GILBERT

I'm absolutely sweating cobs, good grief its hot in here, I'm roasting! I slowly move one leg from under the bedsheets to dangle my foot off the mattress edge because, well, that usually cools you down, right? I find myself yet again lying wide-awake tossing and turning to get comfortable, desperately trying not to wake up fully. Damn it, it's too late, I'm slowly emerging one limb at a time from underneath the covers to cool down.

I can feel my hips are aching, my knee joints are sore from lack of movement and my lower back is in so much pain. Oh for god's sake, I may as well just get up, because now I'm wide awake and every pain sensor in my body has activated. Not only that my overactive brain has now switched to that all important question of *"do I need a wee or not?"* and then it has swiftly digressed to planning today's tasks for me. I'm now remembering that email that annoyed me yesterday I

187

need to send a considered polite response to, that website I saved an article from to read later and that policy document I need to finish writing, the meetings scheduled in my diary I need to attend, the book I need to format and the audiobook I need to load to ACX, the list is long and I'm adding to it with every passing minute. It's 3am, it's fine, I may as well get up now as I'm well and truly awake.

I can say with honesty, that this is my reality, at least five out of seven nights a week – this is me! I'm sure there are many of you nodding as you read this and recognising the pattern, I'm not alone in this. I know I'm not alone; I see your green *'active'* lights on social media as I'm drinking my first brew of the day. Some of you even post *'is anyone else in the wide-awake club'*. Some of you are just going to bed as I'm getting up, and some of you live on the other side of the world so you are in different time zones ahead of and behind me.

It's now 4:45am, I have been awake for 2 hours, I'm drinking my second mug of coffee and I have been reflecting on life since I wrote my chapter in "Permission" of July 2021, what has happened since then? Oh my, where do I start!

As I sit here, exhausted from my constant lack of sleep night after night, I wonder if this is it for me or if I'll ever find myself sleeping through the night again. I'm certain, once my second mug of coffee kicks in I will be fine.

Recently, I have regressed to a similar sleep pattern which resembles that of a new-born baby. I'm 51 years old, perhaps it's the menopause or perhaps it's all the stress I'm experi-

DON'T JUST RISE, SHINE!

encing in my life or maybe I just don't need that much sleep anymore.

I'm not going to stick a medical label on it, I'm just going to accept for my own sanity, this is normal for me. I function well most days, in fact, I don't just function, I have an insane capacity for delivery and output in all areas of my life; I high perform.

In this chapter I am going to try and explain how I find the time (I've perhaps already explained that part), the energy, and the motivation to do what I do, despite life's set backs to get the results that I get. I hope it offers a lantern of light to anyone who is suffering adversity in anyway, and demonstrates that your choices and actions ultimately lead to what happens next.

Choose wisely!

I'm going to spend today's early hours writing, they won't be wasted by just lying-in bed annoyed that I'm awake or scrolling TikTok on my phone (for complete transparency, I often scroll TikTok, more on that later).

Here is my first high performing pointer, whenever you find yourself saying '*I don't have time*' I'd like you to go and look in the mirror and do the red face test. Try telling yourself to your own face you don't have time. Be honest with yourself and reflect on how you spend your twenty-four hours each day. Is that statement 100% true? Are you trying to lie to yourself? Come on who are you kidding!

You have probably realised by now that my days are very long. I find myself with more hours on my hands than most people and this enables me to appear to the average person as some kind of work machine

1. because I rarely sleep for more than 4 hours at a time
2. because when I'm awake I invest almost all of my time and energy into my work.

I've been this way for as long as I can remember. It helps me to forget the enormous amounts of stress and adversity I have to handle on a daily basis, it might not sound enormous for some of you but to me it feels that way. And just when I think it's over, life throws me some more, it's like an adverse event Groundhog Day, I'm still not sure what lesson it is I meant to be learning. I'm hoping one day I figure it out and manage to break the cycle.

People talk about and we often hear of, work life balance, I've read articles and listened to podcasts suggesting eight hours sleep, eight hours working, and eight hours spent for family and personal activity is a great balance. Except for me this notion couldn't be any further from the truth, I much prefer work, life, harmony. The facts are, we are all different and what is good and fulfilling for one person as an ideal balance or harmony is not right for another, in fact it can be quite stressful that you don't fit into the category. It can lead you to wondering if there is something wrong with you.

It's probably time to introduce myself, I'm Jo Gilbert, wife, mum of three, nanni to two beautiful and clever grandsons, I'm a three times No1 best-selling author, I have worked in the UK energy markets for twenty-two years, I am CEO and Founder of CUBES and the Butterfly House Foundation [mycubes.uk], Founder of Audio and Co, a podcast and audiobook production company [www.audioandco.com] and I also work freelance in publishing with my best friend Abigail Horne, I format all shapes and sizes of books including this one, with Authors and Co [www.author-sandco.pub].

I have a very busy work schedule, so the fact I hardly sleep actually helps! A little bit of back story is perhaps needed from my autobiography to help you get a sense of my adverse life and why I have chosen to name this chapter the way I have, so rather than repeat what I have already written I have provided the book descriptor.

STRENGTH AND POWER

Breaking Through Adversity

Disrupt Your Destiny, By Disrupting Your Reality

I find it so frustrating and confusing when people say to me 'OMG you're so lucky' my usual response is to politely smile while having a quiet split-second memory flashback of why I don't perceive this state-ment to be true. Strength and Power takes you on a journey through my life and describes all of the setbacks and adversity I have faced. Some of you may be facing right now – including losing a loved one to cancer, domestic violence, rape, homelessness, being unemployed and on benefits, divorce, being a single parent, serious illness, debt, fuel poverty to name a few. I'll share with you my quiet split-second thoughts when people say to me 'OMG you're so lucky.' I don't believe it was because of luck I am where I am today, I guess I found a profound Strength and Power to keep moving forward with determination, and I believe you can too.

OK so now I think you are pretty much up to date with who I am and my background. So let's dive into my chapter *'Don't Just Rise, Shine!'*

After the launch of my book in May 2018, I actually did one of the bravest things I have ever done in my life. I completely downsized my life into 3 suitcases, sold everything I owned or gave it away, boarded a plane to Lanzarote and waved goodbye to my over commercialised, sickly life in the UK.

I was heading for a new life in the sunshine, I had reached that point in my life where money, hadn't brought me the life I expected it would. The houses, the fancy sports cars, the holidays, the clothes, all the gadgets, all of the things, were nice of course they were, but I wasn't happy, in fact I'd go as far as to say I was deeply depressed and always ill. I had begun to resent my success and how much I earned. I was also battling health issues from diagnosed kidney disease, I am susceptible to airborne viruses, causing recurring kidney

DON'T JUST RISE, SHINE!

infections and UTI's leading me to have a brush with sepsis on two occasions.

So, everything, and I mean everything got scaled right back, if it didn't fit in to one of the suitcases it wasn't coming with me. I had spent quite a lot of time in self development and trained in NLP and mindfulness and meditation plus other topics like hypnosis. I had decided to hang up my energy sector hat and do something new and completely removed from the corporate career I had at this point, enjoyed for eighteen years. So, I stepped into a new career in business coaching and mentoring.

I have worked so hard all my life, making incredible sacrifices, the biggest one that haunts me is not seeing my children grow up as I was always working and providing, so I missed out on so much with them. I can never get that time back. It's not that I chose my career over my children, I chose not wanting to be poor, and I didn't want them to go without, and not wanting to be poor or considered a failure was and still is my biggest fear and motivation in life.

What a roller coaster it has been, I haven't shared this before other than with my closest friends and family, but I think actually writing this out now is helping me to heal and may help others to avoid the same mistakes I have made especially if they consider moving abroad.

The darkest of clouds has burdened me ever since arriving in Lanzarote and more recently my worst fears have come about in what can only be described as a major crisis point in my life.

In August 2018 as I was boarding a flight back to the Uk to see a consultant at the hospital breast clinic, after discovering a lump in my right boob; I saw a post on Facebook market place and in the confusion of trying to find my boarding pass, I accidentally triggered an auto message 'is this villa still forsale?' to the vendor.

I then got a call from a woman, who was acting as a proxy, power of attorney and estate agent for the gentleman who owned the villa, who's wife had recently died. After viewing the villa on my return from the Uk, I agreed to buy it. I transferred over a large lump sum for a deposit and a few weeks later in the October, after agreeing contracts with the owner and the estate agent, we got the keys to move in. There was a snag however, we couldn't legally complete the purchase at the Notary as the villa was subject to probate as no *'will'* had been in place when this man's wife had died.

We were assured there was nothing to worry about, cases like this are quite common, so we agreed to a *'rent to buy contract'* on the villa until the end of the year while this was sorted. All the money we had paid in would be deducted from the final amount we needed to pay when we completed the purchase at the notary, it sounded straight forward and fair enough.

Now, what I need you to understand at this point is we have contracts in place and paid a hefty deposit, thousands of

DON'T JUST RISE, SHINE!

euros. If we didn't go ahead with the purchase we would lose all the money we had paid in so far. Whilst probate was being dealt with, we got a small mortgage in place ready to complete the mortgage was actually smaller than the deposit we had already paid. The three month contract expired, so we chased up on what was going on. We were told there was an inheritance issue, and the owner needed to go to court to ask a judge to grant him permission to sell the villa on behalf of his son as well; we were once again asked to be patient. We have the villa so we weren't to worry everything was fine.

A couple of weeks passed and we were asked to provide another sizeable chunk of money because the owner needed it for a deposit for his new house, plus we needed to start paying the owners mortgage on our villa, which we did, although it always felt like we were being forced, and threatened into handing money over for the owner. We were in too deep to say no at this point, so I was left little choice.

Now when I say the level of anxiety myself and my husband have been subjected to for the past three and a half years in dealing with this villa purchase has been horrendous, it's probably, no, definitely, an understatement. The whole experience has been vile, you read about these things in magazines or see them on TV but you never once think it could happen to you. Not one thing went right for us, everyday was a new battle, with paperwork, residency, social security, even getting a doctor or dentist was an ordeal, I still don't have one. My husband even had all of his paperwork stolen, a week after he had finally got his sorted out. His passport, driving licence, residencia, wallet, everything taken, so he had to start all over again.

We would try to get on with our lives and enjoy the experience of living in the sunshine, and some days we did manage to put what we were going through to the back of our minds and enjoy life, as if we were on holiday. Mostly though, it was always there, eating away at us, I can't remember a day where I didn't talk about it or think about it. The villa we had virtually paid for, legally still wasn't ours, yet our funds in the hundreds of thousands at this point, had all but been taken. Months would pass between hearing from the estate agent, and when we did hear from her, we were both on pins because that usually came with another demand for more money for the owner.

We were fed bullshit story after bullshit story for three and a half years by the woman who the owner had appointed to sell the villa for him, while he had moved back to his home country. If covid hadn't of happened we would probably have discovered what we now know sooner.

Not being able to travel back to visit family and friends didn't help. I wasn't in control of anything going on in my life and it was crippling me mentally.

In January 2021 all of the new rules for Brexit kicked in and I still wasn't a resident of Spain, if this wasn't sorted by the end of March, I would need to leave the island for 180 days. My Uk driving licence was about to become void if I didn't retake a test in Spain and get a European licence. So many things I had been trying to resolve for three years and I now had 3 months to sort them out or would be forced to leave my husband and my home behind.

The pressure of everything that was going on, not just with the villa, but with work as well, eventually lead me to have some kind of mental breakdown in February of 2021. My husband and I separated for a few weeks because I needed to be alone and process everything, remember who I was, find my strength, it's what I do. I need to be alone, sleep, listen to music, work, just get lost outside of the situation I'm in.

I was the one making the decisions regarding the villa purchase, so the weight of everything was of course a heavy burden to carry. I should have listened to people warning me of dealing with that women. I should have seen the red flags, in all honesty I did see them, but, because I loved the villa so much and the owner insisted that the only way we could buy it was through her, I felt like I had no choice. I had handed over so much money to begin with and so I couldn't back out when even more red flags appeared, I had reached a point of no return.

They were extremely dark days, I thought about ending my own life so many times to make it stop. Not just a thought, I actually planned how over and over, it was so scary to be alone with those thoughts. I didn't keep this to myself as it was so alien to me, I asked for help and admitted I was having strange thoughts. My friend Shaz was my rock, her counsel dragged me from a really dark place and got me walking and talking every morning for two hours before I started work. She helped me to remember everything good in my life. I'm so thankful to her and for the love I have and bond with my family and friends, their voices in my head keeping me going and showing up everyday.

Despite my intention of a career change, I never did leave the energy sector as planned, it's part of who I am, it's like the Uk energy sector is part of my DNA. I was head hunted as soon as I arrived in Lanzarote, the deal was too good to turn down. I had been asked to support easyEnergy in setting up an energy supply company, it was part of Sir Stelios Haji-Ioannou's easyGroup.

Every week for the first year of living in Lanzarote, I would commute to Gatwick airport on a Sunday evening, staying in the easyHotel in East Croyden. I worked in central London Monday to Weds and flew home Thursday morning catching the 6am flight, I also managed to work remotely a couple of days a week. I did this every week until November 2019 a little over a year. Then in January 2020 I moved to support PFP Energy in Preston and again would commute home to Lanzarote at the weekend until March 2020 when the pandemic begun. I also launched a successful coaching and mentoring business for start-ups and micro businesses, which I did part-time, with several clients coming from reading my autobiography.

On top of everything that was going on with the villa purchase these past few years, it would seem it wasn't enough stress, so life dealt me some more recently.

At career level, I have felt the full wrath of the current Uk energy crisis, and at the end of August 2021 I found myself having to inform Ofgem the energy supply company I was running was going to become insolvent. Our wholesale energy provider withdrew our hedged position as wholesale energy costs were spiralling (energy we had bought in advance for our customers at a much lower rate) and they were terminating our contract with immediate effect. This left us exposed to the increasing wholesale markets and meant that they could now sell that energy again at four or five times more than what we had originally paid for it (a massive windfall for wholesalers, at the expense of smaller suppliers and their consumers - You!).

A company with an annual turnover of £108million out of business just like that, I had to put 54 members of staff on notice of redundancy heading into the Christmas period including myself and the company went into a process called SoLR (Supplier of Last Resort) and 80k of our customers were transferred to British Gas. I was devastated for everyone involved including the customers. I knew that by the end of September, once I had appointed the administrators I would be made redundant and lose the majority of my household income just like that.

I went into a complete panic, OMG the villa purchase was due to complete soon surely (a thought I had every week for the past few years) and now I won't have the right amount of payslips to show the bank, or three years of accounts, or they will see a gap in my employment. Shit, if I can't get a mortgage, even though its only small, I'll lose everything. So many panic thoughts.

I was due to speak at Bee Inspired in Manchester at the end of October with @iamthequeenbee Dani Wallace. The truth is I didn't feel very inspiring at that time so I let Dani know I needed to fly home and re-group my thoughts and what I was going to do next to recover my income. Most of my savings had been handed over to buy the villa, the pot of money, our safety net was gone. My fear of becoming homeless, poor, jobless, losing what we had already paid was intense. I could hardly breathe, and I hardly slept in the weeks that followed.

I lashed out my anger and frustration towards the energy regulator Ofgem, and to this day still hold them to blame for the mess the industry was in and the insolvency of thirty-one energy supply companies due to their extremely poor market design and forcing them to sell energy at huge losses. They can lie all they like to mainstream media, telling consumers we were unhedged and poorly run - thirty-one supplier's they were meant to be regulating? If this was true what the hell were Ofgem doing? Had they fallen asleep at the wheel? It's all nonsense and lies, those of us who were used as scape goats, whilst wholesalers were terminating contracts and cashing out hedged positions to resell them, know the truth of what was happening, it was because of Ofgem and government failings they were allowing this to happen. These people are now marking their own homework and trying to fix the mess they created in the first place.

It was a really stressful, but action taking, busy period in my life. It momentarily allowed me to stop worrying about the villa, apart from the slight issue of the mortgage application and lack of income, I was too busy to think about it when working.

I'm not one to sit around waiting for an opportunity to fall in my lap or to throw a pity party. I had bills to pay, so I needed to act quickly in securing investment for my new venture CUBES (Customer Utility Bills Expertly Serviced), which had been in development for ten months at this point, but put on the back burner so many times due to client commitments or something not sitting quite right with me about the operating model or the investors that came forward. I knew the right time would present itself and it did.

I also launched Audio and Co in November 2021, so my work life was really busy and maxed to capacity. Despite everything that was going on in my life at that point, nothing was going to prepare me for what happened next. December 2021, I have got to be honest came very close to breaking me completely. I am strong willed but there is only so much a human can cope with at one time?

I got sent a news article on WhatsApp which was about to shatter my world even further, as if the past few months stress wasn't enough to deal with, life has this magical way of testing me to the maximum limit.

The woman who had been dealing with our villa purchase was been requested by the Prosecutor in Lanzarote for 6 years in jail for 'misappropriation of €67,000 of funds for a property sale' nothing to do with us, this was somebody else's money she had stolen. A warrant has now been issued for her arrest and a 'Wanted' Facebook group set up for all of her victims. When I last checked there were over 200 people in the group, the scale of this is huge.

NEWS UPDATE
ARREST WARRANT ISSUED FOR BRITISH ESTATE AGENT

GAZETTELIFE.COM
Arrest warrant issued for British estate agent – Gazette Life

Time literally stood still whilst I read the article and processed what this could mean for us and our purchase. In simple terms the owner of the villa and his proxy, this con-woman between them have taken my life savings and I am now having to take the owner to court for refusing to sign the villa over to us, because she has done a runner with the majority of the funds I have paid.

The owner has had a third of what I have paid, a lump sum, and monthly payments to more than cover the mortgage. Sadly he is making out I've never paid him a penny towards the purchase, and is now calling my regular mortgage payments 'rent' despite me having a legal contract to buy the villa in place and it clearly stating that all payments will be deducted from the final purchase price! Not only that he thinks it's unfair that the property has increased in value so we should increase our offer! You honestly couldn't make this stuff up, I lost my absolute shit when I read that email from him!

We have never once discussed renting with him or her. I wasn't in the market to rent a villa, I was in the market to buy, he knew that then and he knows that now. He is conve-niently denying any knowledge of it because he doesn't want it to be him who is the victim of her fraud. He would much prefer I lost everything for his mistake of appointing her power of attorney in the first place.

Luckily I have saved all the emails, WhatsApp messages, voice clips and recorded her recent threatening and abusive phone calls, including him accepting our offer and agreeing to his proxy's proposed purchase agreement contract terms.

As it currently stands, I have lost all the money, every cent of it has gone. On top of that, I have received unwelcome communication from the villa owner because I refuse to give him any more money or to move out, why should I, it's my home, I've paid for it! I have also spent thousands more improving and repairing it over the past few years too, so this isn't just about the money they stole, it's much more than that.

For the record, trying to intimidate me almost worked, I almost gave up and walked away, because I had so much going on with work too. I didn't want the threat of nasty people turning up trying to repossess the villa, I didn't want him turning up, or her whilst she is still on the run. I almost retreated back to the Uk, defeated and ready to take on a huge mortgage debt again. The villa doesn't feel like a happy family home anymore, it never really has been. How could it be, it's a constant reminder of what we have already endured to get to this point and what we are continuing to go through.

They are both fraudsters as far as I'm concerned, they took our money under false pretence with no intent to sell the property, they have dragged things on for so long for their own financial gain and reward. He had no legal right without the courts permission to sell the villa in the first place. She worked for and represented him, not me, I had no choice but to deal with her, it's what he told us to do.

I have completed a denouncia for him at the notary. There is now a court case underway, and as everything is in Spanish I have no clue what the hell is going on, apart from being told it could take years to sort out, and in the mean time to go and enjoy the villa (that's easier said than done). It's costing me an arm and a leg in legal fees. I have quite literally had my home stolen from me, I am in limbo for the foreseeable future and can do nothing until the court decide. If I move out now I may lose everything, it's not worth the risk.

So, I have decided to take back control. My beautiful life, in Lanzarote never actually materialised they had taken that too with their selfish actions. Well, not anymore! What we got was a living nightmare, I am now going to remind myself why I moved here in the first place and what an amazing beautiful island we live on.

The money we have handed over, I have now mentally written off, so if we do ever get any of it back it will be a bonus. For now it's filed as a lesson learned. I am staying put, I was legally advised to do so, it's my home. I refuse to let him take back possession of it, unless a court tells me otherwise. If I do ever have the mis-fortune of coming face to face with that woman ever again she will be wishing she never met me because I will literally drag her ass to court myself and see her put in jail.

Top tip:

DEAL WITH PROPERLY QUALIFIED LAWYERS WHENEVER YOU BUY A PROPERTY!

I haven't crumbled this time, I refuse to, they haven't broken me down. What they have stolen between them isn't just money, it's me missing seeing my children grow up, its endless hours working my arse off, it endless commutes on the motorway and being stuck in traffic, its missing family events, it's missing holidays, its living away from home. They haven't just stolen my home, they have stolen all of those things from my past which that money represented.

They are now also attempting to steal what should be my future, my peace of mind, retired at 55, mortgage and debt free, living in the sunshine in my favourite place in the world. I will achieve this, the route might be different, however I refuse to allow them to be in control anymore.

She phoned me when the article was published shouting about people I'd never even heard of, crying and angry saying everything that was being said about her was untrue, threatening me, telling me I couldn't go to a lawyer. She maintained her lies of three and a half years in those phone calls, right up until her disappearance on 17th December 2021.

She said, she had considered taking her own life, crying to me "she has a daughter". Well, I have all of those things too, and neither her nor the owner considered my family, my feelings in any of this with their web of lies! You can't just take peoples money, lie and steal and expect a sob story and that crying down the phone will fix things.

"I have decided instead of being a victim, I would rise, not just rise I'm fucking shining!

You can steal my money, but you will never take my determination to win, and as long as I have forgiveness in my heart, love and happiness will shine through always"

— JO GILBERT

I'm trying to find the lessons in everything that has happened these past few years, one I never need to search to far for is this;

 "Everyone goes down a road that they're not supposed to go down. You can do two things from it. You can keep going down that road and go to a dark place. Or you can turn and go up the hill and go to the top - try to go to the top."

— JULIAN EDELMAN

It's been a chaotic 8 months, and despite tackling huge amounts of adversity I managed to find the opportunities, to find a new hill and I'm trying so bloody hard to get to the top. It's a trek uphill I'm willing to take.

I got made redundant on the last day of September. On the first day of October I was appointed Founder and CEO of

CUBES and The Butterfly House Foundation. I had secured the investment, I needed.

I became an employee straight away so there was no gap in my employment history and no change in my salary. My brand, the ideas, the IPR, everything, I have handed over to the investors in exchange for a salary and agreement that the profits of the company go to a new charity with causes very close to my heart. We are all in agreement we will make a difference to peoples lives.

I have always wanted to be in a position to give something back, and despite my own financial setback regarding the villa, I didn't want this to change my vision and plans for the profits of CUBES, the need for CUBES and Butterfly House is far bigger than my needs will ever be. Far bigger than my fears, so I'm showing up, stepping outside of my comfort zone and doing this!

Every penny of the money from **CUBES** will be used to create local centres designed to support the vulnerable.

Our **'Butterfly Houses'** will begin by providing four sets of tools and support:

🦋 **Accommodation**

Giving shelter, warmth, food and importantly security for those who need it.

🦋 **Support Framework**

Offering the planned and reactive emotional support needed by some of the most vulnerable.

𝖂 Educational Support

Assisting with identifying, applying and securing a variety of key qualifications.

𝖂 Job Support

Helping with access to a range of apprenticeships, full and part-time roles through our partners.

We will also run bespoke neighbourhood initiatives, where we see the opportunity to support local communities.

Focus, intuition, and sheer determination have brought me to this point. I would encourage everyone to go and find out more about CUBES because you will not only benefit from it, people who need support will benefit from it too! Let us all be the changes makers together.

High Performance top tip! Do what makes your heart sing!

If you are struggling to get out of bed and show up in your personal life or your business, then something perhaps needs to change. Find something like I have that is bigger than me, a *'why'* to make your heart sing and you will never work a day in your life again.

Money is no longer a motivator for me, it's brought me nothing but trouble and heartache if I'm honest, so I'm glad any profits we generate will now go to good causes instead. I don't live a lavish life, I live a modest but comfortable one, however I know only too well what its like to not be in such a privileged position. Remember my fear of being poor is one of my drivers, it stems from my past, my autobiography explains it.

Perhaps I still have money mindset issues to deal with, but until I have, I would rather do good with the money and not let fraudsters benefit from it ever again.

My other company Audio and Co is thriving too and my husband Craig now manages that company for me and has taken over full-time to free me up to focus on CUBES and Butterfly House. In such a short space of time we have already taken on some big hitting clients including Frank Bruno and 60 Years a Fighter, and Katie Hopkins Help!

I said earlier I would come back to TikTok. It is my one social media weakness. I go to bed thinking I'll watch it for a few minutes to unwind before going to sleep. My god you can lose hours on that app watching nonsense. My obsession and I have no plausible explanation for it at all, is watching Dr Pimple Popper I find it really relaxing! If I were to ever be caught procrastinating, I would hazard a guess it would be TikTok that was the culprit.

I'd like to leave you with this final thought, if you face adversity or hardship remember the pain is temporary. You need to take positive action to get you out of the pain and hardship. Burying your head in the sand and crying won't get you a new job, or a new business, or a new house. Hatred

DON'T JUST RISE, SHINE!

towards anyone who has done you wrong will fester and be like a scab you pick daily.

Forgiveness disempowers wrong doers. The other thing that disempowers them is your success.

You need to be a massive action taker, the time is going to pass anyway, and whether you react positively with action, or negatively with 'pity party' both are hard, as the late great Jim Rohn said.

'CHOOSE YOUR HARD!'

Don't let adversity win, it can't sit with us, there are no seats at our table available for it.

ABOUT THE AUTHOR

JO GILBERT

Jo has worked in the UK gas and electricity industry for the past 22 years. She is an entrepreneur and multiple business owner.

In May 2018 Jo became an international #1 Amazon Best Selling Author with her first book on overcoming adversity, 'Strength & Power', later that year securing her second #1 Amazon Best Seller with the collaboration book 'She Who Dares'. In July 2021 Jo Co-authored her third #1 Amazon Best Seller 'Permission'

Jo has launched and supported several UK energy companies to market in her role as an Industry Expert, Business

Strategist and Consultant.

Jo is the CEO and Founder of Customer Utility Bills Expertly Serviced, known simply as CUBES. This brand new consumer champion service launched on 4th of April 2022 for all UK households and Businesses.

You can contact Jo:

Email: jo.gilbert@mycubes.uk

Website: mycubes.uk | www.audioandco.com

Podcast: Lifting the Lid

Socially connect with Jo:

facebook.com/cubesexpert

instagram.com/cubesexpert

linkedin.com/in/cubesExpert

pinterest.com/cubesexpert

twitter.com/cubesexpert

tiktok.com/@cubesexpert

WRITE TO IGNITE

I love to write and I always have.

One year around the mid-90s there was a mega downpour of snow and we were all sent home as the pipes froze at school. The jubilation as we all ran out of school and pretty much the whole school joined with a snowball fight on the field (I'm sure the teachers joined in too) is still ingrained in my memory. We were off school for ages.

Back then there was none of this home-schooling or Zoom lessons; we were free to roam and play and just be. Our whole street joined in with making an igloo on our drive. Well, everyone except me. I was about fourteen and I used the time to start writing my book, '*Lizzie.*' I locked myself away and just wrote. It was my pride and joy and I declared to everyone that I had started writing my book. As the neighbourhood children frolicked and had fun in the snow, I was in the happiest place I could be. However, once GCSEs continued to roll Lizzie and I became distant friends. I often think about her now and would love to reconnect with her but sadly she is trapped in an old floppy disc!

Fear has held me back, stopped me writing and even stopped me dreaming at times. What is your fear? What would you really like to do that you have almost stopped dreaming about?

Bringing together a collaboration of empowered voices and supporting women to write their truth is one of the most powerful ways that I can use my passion and expertise as an English teacher. Helping other women to create impact with their words is something that I feel compelled to do. So let me ask you:

Are you ready to share your story?

To be a voice for other women?

To empower others to share theirs?

Writing is my *first love* and as a published author, English teacher and supporter of women I want to empower and support other women to write their story, but not just to write it; to bring their story to a powerful collective which will be a force for inspiration and empowerment for its reader. You will be fully supported along the way as we plan, write, edit and launch your book and *yes* you will be and *can* be an author!

'From the Ashes; She is Ignited' is collaborative book and mentor programme bringing together women's voices of adversity, loss, survival and empowerment showcasing the light and dark of life, motherhood and the traumas faced by many women.

This can be business related or just your chance to share YOUR journey.

If you would like to chat about joining a future collaboration, please get in touch with Louisa. You can read about future projects here:

https://mamasignited.co.uk/from-the-ashes-she-is-ignited/

REFERENCES

2. THE SCIENCE OF HAPPINESS

1. Glennon Doyle, podcast 'We can do hard things'

Ingram Content Group UK Ltd.
Milton Keynes UK
UKHW020112010623
422666UK00002B/13/J